MAKING LOVE SAFE

FOUNDATIONS OF LOVE

LANGUAGE OF LOVE

LIMITS OF LOVE

By

PHILIP F. GUINSBURG, PH.D.

LUANNE F. OVERTON, M.A.

This book is a work of non-fiction. Names and places have been changed to protect the privacy of all individuals.

ISBN: 1-4107-6439-7 (e-book)
ISBN: 1-4107-6440-0 (Paperback)

Library of Congress Control Number: 2003094267

This book is printed on acid free paper.

Printed in the United States of America
Bloomington, IN

1stBooks – rev. 07/08/03

DEDICATION

This book is dedicated to our mothers, Elena F. Guinsburg and Lee Overton. They were our first relationships and the love and support they have shown us have touched every aspect of our lives. Thank you for teaching us the real safety of love.

ACKNOWLEDGEMENTS

It would not have been possible to write this book without the help of many people. First, we would like to thank our spouses, Debrah Guinsburg and Lynn Blair, who have been both supportive and understanding of what this project has meant to us.

We also want to thank the colleagues who initially reacted to and helped construct the early phases of the book, including Dr. Jack Mulgrew, Dr. Ken Nunnelly, Lisa Davis, Scott Haram, Bob True, and Susan Ludwig.

Dr. Thomas and Julie Guinsburg, Debrah Guinsburg, and Gregory Smith all deserve shouts of praise and recognition for the many hours they spent reading and correcting the various versions of this book. We would never have been able to publish our work without the careful editing they provided.

We want to thank Lyn Probst and DeVina Shields, who patiently made copies and always believed in our efforts. We owe a debt of gratitude to Dr. Michael Gatton, who referred us to 1st Books Library and to J.R. Harris and Jill Weimer, our contacts at 1st Books Library, for patiently working with us to get the manuscript published.

Dr. Guinsburg would like to thank Dr. Paul Wright, an inspiration from graduate school, who motivated him to explore opposite sex relationships, both romantic and platonic. Finally, we need to acknowledge the many couples we have worked with over the years. We have learned from and been inspired by their struggles to make love safe.

Photo on back cover taken by Mark Tsai.

INTRODUCTION

When we started working as co-therapists in 1976, we were frustrated by the limited impact we could have on couples who were trying to strengthen their relationships. There were excellent methodologies and techniques available to identify problems. We would listen to the points of contention, negotiate rough spots and assist in, what we saw as short term solutions. Yet, we did not feel that we had the tools or ability to help a couple develop the strengths that could endure over time and bridge the many transitions that a long-term relationship faces.

Listening and trying to really hear what couples were asking for, we turned back to work that we had both done in graduate school. In our respective master's theses and dissertation we had explored various aspects of relationships; dimensions of perceived marital satisfaction and the differences between platonic and heterosexual relationships. Not surprisingly, we saw that the relationship dimensions that factored into perceived marital satisfaction changed over the years, moving from early romantic ideals to a more solid sense of emotional acceptance. More interesting were the differences we saw between platonic relationships and romantic relationships. Aside from the inherent sexual focus of the two types of relationships, our research showed that platonic friends felt that their relationship were more useful and they felt a greater sense of acceptance than in their romantic relationships. There was a greater sense of safety in the platonic relationships. What was behind the lack of emotional safety that we saw in so many of the couples with whom we worked? What were the factors that drew individuals into a romantic involvement versus a platonic involvement? How were the expectations of the two relationships different? Pulling from what we had researched and with these questions still hanging, we found a direction for working with couples.

People enter into a romantic relationship clouded by expectations, both stated and unstated. When these expectations are not met, the individuals are hurt, angry and unwilling to continue to risk further rejection. They focus on the differences and try to make their partner who they thought they should be. We recognized that couples really don't know what else to do. Nowhere are they taught what they might expect from an emotionally healthy and supportive commitment. We also needed to develop some sort of communication framework, a language that would help couples express what they needed and wanted emotionally and that could be translated into the behaviors that make up our daily interactions. Finally, we had to address how couples could deal with some inherent limits that individuals bring into a relationship and recognize those factors, which no amount of love or caring will fix.

In working with hundreds of couples in the last twenty-five years, we have answered our questions and developed the tools that can strengthen most relationships. We have written this book in the same style that we have used in our work; simple, straight-forward, presenting questions to explore and encouraging an interactive safe environment in which a couple might grow. We hope that you, the reader, will discover more about yourself, your partner, and your relationship as you read this book. Have fun with it, use it as a point of conversation and sharing with your partner. Keep moving through the hard parts and remember the goal is to make love safe.

MAKING LOVE SAFE

People are often confused and puzzled by what is happening in their relationships. They know something does not feel right but they are not sure what is wrong. Self-help books, designed to help people understand their relationships often complicate the issues. Being in a relationship takes **work**, but it does not have to be **hard**.

In this book, we talk about relationships in a down to earth, common sense manner. In fact, much of what you will read may seem pretty obvious once we begin to look at what people really want in a relationship and apply a simple approach to help them get it. Any relationship (whether we are talking about a marriage, a friendship, or a long term committed relationship) where the individuals involved can flourish, must feel "safe." A feeling of safety comes from knowing what is going on and what to expect.

In part one, Foundations of Love, we try to provide you with a blueprint or a model for how a relationship could feel. A loving relationship does take work but there are many reasons to invest the time and energy that is required. Often we have worked with couples who have lost the joy and rewards they once felt in their relationship and have turned to counseling for the sake of the children or simply to avoid divorce. Their relationship is no longer safe and the expectations they once had have been dashed. In this first part we will look at the romantic expectations and hopes, both known and unknown, that pull one into a relationship. We will also address ten different emotional rewards you can realistically hope to achieve from a relationship if you work for them.

In part two, The Language of Love, we give you the building blocks and tools to achieve the blueprint of the relationship we describe in the first section. We develop a simple formula that combines the emotional states that provide safety with operational steps formed from behaviors.

We use this simple formula in sixteen different emotional need areas. As a couple works together to define their unique needs in these sixteen areas, they create a language or way to communicate as a couple that allows them to understand and get what they need from their partner and relationship.

No plan is without its limitations. In part three of this book, The Limits of Love, we will address some difficult relationship issues that can limit what one might be able to expect from their partner or achieve in their relationship. In exploring different specific topics such as finances, infidelity, religious involvement, physical violence, alcohol and drug use and others we help couples explore their individual positions and the "bottom lines" in their relationships. In working with couples for over thirty years we recognize that there are certain stances or responses that do not change for an individual. These areas need to be identified and understood. However, rather than creating road blocks, knowing the limits of your partner can help create the boundaries of safety. Just as in the other sections of the book, part three creates safety by clarifying what is going on and what to expect.

We hope that you will find Making Love Safe an interesting and easy book to read. Beyond that we hope you will use the book as a tool to explore your individual needs and the needs you have as a couple. Throughout the book we have used an on-going case example of a composite couple to bring the many topics we discuss into the realm of the daily relationship. We also pose questions in each section to help you explore your own responses and stimulate conversation with your partner. In some sections we have included examples of responses that we have derived from our many years of working with real life couples in counseling. Making love and relationships safe is not a theoretical exercise. It does take work and will touch all aspects of your life together. However, the work is worth it because in discovering more about yourself and your partner you can find a love that will last.

PART ONE

THE FOUNDATIONS OF LOVE

A lot of people have unrealistic expectations about relationships. In almost a quarter of a century of work with married couples, we have run into a wide range of expectations that people bring into their relationships. In many cases, the expectations just set both people up to be let down. What we will do in this simple book is look at some of the unrealistic expectations that people place at their partner's feet when they fall in love, and explore why those expectations can't be met. We will also identify ten specific expectations that people can reasonably achieve in their relationships. The goal is to provide you with a sense of what is going on in your relationship and what to expect. We want to help you find safety in your relationship.

THE SECRETS OF FALLING IN LOVE: WHAT WE ARE REALLY LOOKING FOR

THE LIST WE KNOW

Most people think they know what attracted them to their partner. They can list characteristics or qualities they are looking for in a mate; what many refer to as "the package" or "the list." This list includes things like body type, hair and eye color, skin color, height, age range, profession, religion, and social background. Yet in reality what people are aware they are looking for is only part of the story. Much of what attracts us to another individual are qualities of which we are not consciously aware.

The conscious package we know about comes from what we are used to, and what we have been taught to look for. Parents, grandparents, teachers, religious leaders, siblings all have their input to our list of what is important to look for in a mate. We are supposed to choose someone of a certain socio-economic level, educational level, religion, vocation, and look. If you look in any of the singles listings, they have even come up with code systems to simplify the "list": **SWM, NS, ISO, S/D, WF, 30-45, NS.**

The things on "the list" do make the beginning of a relationship easier, simply because the qualities on the list are familiar and you don't have to start from scratch. If nothing else, you can talk about the things you have in common from the list. It is easier to talk to someone who has the same background and educational level. It is easier to connect physically and sexually if your body types are compatible and you "look good" together. Sunday mornings are less of a challenge if you and your partner have similar religious backgrounds and experiences.

Sometimes we are drawn to a certain quality or characteristic because it is the opposite of our own life experiences. For example, if you were raised in poverty, wealth and financial success may be top on your list. If you are an only child with no cousins you might want to be with a partner who has a large extended family. These "differences" actually match an experience we have always dreamed about but have never had, so in their own way they also are familiar.

- Can you write down "the list" that you had when you were looking for a partner? (physical type, social background, educational level, religious background, common interests)

- Do you know what your partner's list was?

-Can you identify some of the outside sources that contributed to your list/ your partner's list? (mother, father, church, peers)

-How many of these characteristics are in the person you are involved with at present?

-Which characteristics seem to have dropped out over the years or have just changed form?

THE LIST WE DON'T KNOW

People spend a lot of time planning who they want to be with, when in fact the person they plan to be with is usually not the person with whom they end up. Have you ever gone out with a person who matched all the criteria on "the list", but just didn't do anything for you sexually or romantically? There are five different factors that affect whom we are attracted to that we are not aware of on a conscious level. These five areas actually overpower the obvious reasons that attract us to somebody and don't change much over time. Because these are sub-conscious, even people who leave a painful relationship often find that their next relationships are actually similar choices in different packages.

1. OPPOSITES ATTRACT

Part of what helps a relationship feel alive is when the individuals are different enough to provide stimulating interaction. A relationship requires two people who are separate and unique. If you are with someone who is an emotional clone, the spark or challenge of relating is lost, both in the everyday interaction and in the bedroom.

We are actually drawn to people who are different from us in very discreet ways. These differences don't contradict the external similarities that exist on our conscious list. Rather they exist on a less obvious level and are expressed subtly in our interactions. For example, two people may both enjoy "the outdoors"; however to one that might mean "roughing it for the weekend" and for the other a stroll in the park qualifies as an "outdoor activity." Or two people might both love the movies, but one wants to discuss and critique the movie while the other likes movies solely for the entertainment value and the popcorn.

Many new couples would disagree with the premise that we are drawn to someone who is different from us, because when you "fall in love" you feel like you have finally found someone who is just like you. Often people describe their romantic partner as a "soul mate" and feel like they are cut from the same cloth. However, our work with couples bears out that people are usually attracted to someone who is different from themselves.

As couples become aware of the underlying personality differences, these differences become a source for disagreements and fights. Our legal system has even validated "Irreconcilable Differences" as grounds for divorce. When couples divorce, however, the individuals often find that the next person they get involved with is just as different from them as their previous partner, and usually in the same ways.

There is no specific explanation for why one is drawn to another who is different. One can assume that people are drawn to someone different because there are advantages to being involved with another with different skills, capabilities, assets, and outlooks. Some theorists would say that we feel more "complete" when we are with someone who can add to our assets and skills. Others would say that the differences allow for tension and conflict to occur, which is viewed as a necessary component of sexual attraction and excitement. The differences that each partner brings to a relationship add to what we know and provide a different point of view. The differences can add the spice that flavors a relationship.

Let us introduce Tom and Mary. They are a composite couple, a couple that most people will be able to relate to in one instance or another. We will use Tom and Mary to illustrate how some of the issues we discuss actually look within the context of a relationship.

Tom and Mary have been married for ten years. They met in college and come from a similar socio-economic background. Both state that when they got married they felt that they had met their "soul mate" and were alike in many, many ways. Over the course of ten years they have come to recognize some very specific differences. Tom is more outgoing and spontaneous. Mary is introverted, more self- disciplined, and more emotionally responsive. Often, Tom and Mary would fight over how much they should socialize, concerns about money, and differences in emotional needs.

- How are you and your partner alike in the ways you respond to things? How are you different?

- How are you and your partner alike or different in how you view money; how you view leisure time?

- What are the ways in which you deal with these differences?

2. WE MARRY OUR PARENTS

Most people swear that they will never marry someone who was like their parent in one way or another. For example, as children we might promise ourselves that we will never choose someone who is weak and passive like our mother or someone who is angry and a bully like our father. Actually, the child usually ends up putting characteristics that are the opposite of their parent on "the list" they know, so this child consciously looks for a partner who is assertive (unlike mother) and fair (unlike father).

The characteristics and accompanying interactions of all of our earliest caregivers (our parents, siblings, grandparents, hired caregivers) come together to form a composite representation of the relationship that feels familiar. It is this factor of attraction that may explain why one person is more desirable than another. A person who seems to have the composite characteristics and familiar interactions reaches some part in our inner makeup that says, "This is the way a relationship is supposed to feel".

Because our earliest interactions have been molded by the characteristics of our primary caregivers, we are often most comfortable being with the people who possess these qualities. However, many of these same familiar qualities were not particularly good for us as children and remain equally difficult for us to deal with as adults. Take for example children who grew up with an alcoholic parent. With all sincerity they swear that they will never marry an alcoholic- and they don't. They involve themselves with a partner who does not drink, but relationally is inconsistent, and emotionally absent, with significant mood swings. No, they did not marry an alcoholic, but they matched the pattern of interaction.

Some of the composite characteristics may not be dominant in those to whom we are drawn, yet we bring those characteristics out in our partner because of our own expectations that they will be there. We are all able to mold an interaction, whether we know it or not, by the response set we expect; the old "self-fulfilling prophecy." If, for example, we are mistrusting and suspicious of our partner all the time, the partner will react to the lack of trust by distancing himself or herself and often seeking a more comfortable interaction elsewhere which then reinforces the original suspicion.

Tom complained that his wife had changed over the course of their marriage. He stated that when they first got married, she seemed even tempered and fairly passive. After ten years she was now quite explosive with him over certain issues. When Tom reflected on his parents, he realized that his father was one of those people who would explode out of nowhere. Tom brought this expectation into his marriage and projected that response onto his agreeable wife constantly questioning the sincerity of her easy-going nature. It may have taken ten years, but Mary finally gave Tom the response he was continually looking for when he questioned her even temper.

- Which characteristics of your parents and childhood caretakers do you see in your current partner? Are they angry, absent, caring, critical, playful, helpful, distant.....?

- How similar are you to the person/persons who raised your partner?

- Can you identify the characteristics of your caregivers you have managed to bring out or create in your partner?

-How many of the characteristics of the people who raised you do you see in the close friends that you have?

3. WE FEEL EACH OTHER'S PAIN

We are unconsciously attracted to individuals who have experienced a similar hurt or unpleasantness in childhood. The specific event or events that created the hurt may not be the critical draw, but when we meet someone who carries a familiar wound, it seems that they know exactly how we feel in the deepest corners of our souls. In some ways they probably do, particularly if they were hurt in similar ways.

The childhood hurt or wounding does not have to come in the same form or from the same circumstance, but simply has to affect the child with a similar painful or negative feeling. For example, you may be drawn to another who felt emotionally abandoned as a child, just as you did. Although you may have been separated from a parent due to divorce, your partner may have lost a parent due to death, illness, or addiction. Other common negative feelings that we carry with us from childhood may include feeling rejected or unloved, feeling unacceptable or worthless, feeling shameful or not good enough.

Even though two people may have the same type of hurt, how they responded or learned to cope with the childhood hurt will vary. For example, when a child feels rejected or not good enough, he or she may defend against the pain by deciding that he or she doesn't care what other people think. Another child who feels rejected or not good enough, may devote all of his energy trying to win the approval of others. The response is different but the wounding is the same. The difference will not affect the pull of attraction but may contribute to the differences that make relationships interesting and allow the feeling of connectedness. Being with a partner who shares a common wounding as a child has its "good news" and its "bad news". The "good news" is the feeling of being totally understood on that deepest level. With this common emotional experience, couples can be very supportive and accepting, generating a healing environment for each other. The "bad news" is that this individual who knows your pain, also knows how to hurt you. They know the path to the vulnerable spots and they know the "buttons to push" once they get there. So the person who has the potential to be your greatest comfort also has the potential to wield the most painful blow.

Tom and Mary both came from childhood situations where they felt "unloved." Tom responded to this wounding by wanting to find someone to "give his love to" as a way to cover up his feeling of being unlovable. Mary responded to her childhood wounding by keeping a distance from love, choosing rather not to feel it than to risk losing love. Without a conscious awareness of these issues, Tom and Mary have inadvertently reinforced the childhood wounds. Tom tried to give "all his love" to Mary, who was not open to receiving it. Feeling his love rejected, Tom withdrew from Mary reinforcing her belief that loving relationships cannot last.

-What do you think was the main disappointment or hurt from your childhood?

-Is this hurt or disappointment similar to that of your partner or do you even know?

-Has the interaction of you and your partner made your hurt better or worse?

4. WE WANT TO MAKE THAT SPECIAL DIFFERENCE

Most of us would like to be beneficial to others in a certain way. Some of us want to be teachers, some of us caregivers, some of us saviors, some of us providers. Some just want to be catalysts. The pull to have a particular type of role or provide a certain benefit to others usually is formulated in our upbringing. For example if you grow up in a household where one of the parents has an addictive or emotional problem, the child will often grow up with an urge to "fix" someone or find the special behaviors that will make another happy. If you come from a fairly large family and you are the youngest, you will likely grow to be an adult who seeks others who will listen to your ideas or will enjoy the "teacher" in you. Finally, if you come from a family where it was hard to show or give affection, you may grow up with an urge to share your love with others who can appreciate it.

Most people are not consciously aware of how they want to be beneficial to others, nor do we look deeper to see how we want to make a difference to the people with whom we are most intimately involved. Being involved with a partner who needs us in a special way touches our sense of purpose and identity. It is a powerful but usually unknown pull.

People may be drawn together in an unspoken pact of how they will fit into each other's need to make a difference. The teacher will find the student. The special confidante will find the stoic introvert. The caregiver will find the needy. This aspect of attraction creates a unique spin to the evolution of relationships. If these roles all play out then the student will learn and no longer need the teacher in the same way. The stoic introvert will get in touch with his or her need to connect and will reach out to others beyond his or her special confidante. Hopefully people grow and can move out of their special role, but often they don't. Couples tend to bind each other into the roles that they themselves need and inhibit growth and development that may threaten the balance of this script. Unconscious assumptions play a large part in this aspect of attraction. We usually don't share how we want to make a difference to our partner, because we don't clearly know ourselves. However, we all assume that our partner will in fact need us in this special and unspoken way. In the early stages of attraction, when both people are focused solely on making the other happy (so they won't go away), it appears that we will be willing to take on just about any role.

Later in the relationship, as we are becoming more aware of the differences, we may find that our partner really does not need us in this special way. This need to feel that we have a special impact often runs deeper than stated commitments and we will gravitate to some person or persons who can appreciate the impact we want to have. Usually people will seek to have this need met in their work environment or with their children. If that is not possible then they will likely seek out another potential partner.

Tom and Mary each had a specific agenda of how they wanted to make a difference to the other. Tom was the youngest of four and was really looking for an adult partner who would listen to him and look up to his ideas. Mary was somewhat of an individualist as a child and was always questioned when she wanted to do something different from the others. As an adult she was drawn to Tom because she sensed he would appreciate her strong sense of loyalty to him. However, Mary's individuality challenged Tom's need to feel valued. Tom was not able to appreciate Mary's loyalty and actually questioned it every time he felt let down by her.

-What do you think is the main way you want to have a beneficial impact on your partner?

-What do you believe is the most important thing you need to appreciate about your partner?

-How often do you reinforce your partner for being beneficial in these ways and how often do you feel a sense of appreciation from your partner for what you offer him or her?

5. WE WANT OUR OWN PRIVATE "LOVE STORY"

We are drawn to somebody who will fit into our fantasy of what a couple ought to be like. Most of us have an image of how a couple ought to function together. We develop this image from watching TV, our own parents, and parents of close friends. Different marital scenarios include couples who do most everything together, or couples who are basically separate and spend little time together; couples who are totally in agreement and are harmonious, or couples who fight a lot, couples where one is clearly in a position of authority over the other, and couples where the two people operate as complete equals.

Mary's family did not do a lot of things together. Her parents did not really work together as a couple and would often go out at night separately. Tom came from a family where his parents socialized frequently, had similar hobbies and interests, and did most everything together. When Tom and Mary fell in love, Tom assumed that Mary would want to do most things together. Mary assumed that Tom would be comfortable with them having separate interests.

-Before you got married, what was your fantasy of married life?

-Do you know what your partner's fantasy was?

-How similar were these fantasies?

When we fall in love with somebody, we simultaneously make all sorts of assumptions about this other person without having any source of reality on which to base our assumptions. For example, we might make the assumption that the person we are drawn to is just like us, which may or may not be true. We assume that the object of our affection needs us in just the way we want to be needed. We assume that they have the same vision of a romantic involvement that we have. Romantic love has the potential to lead to real chaos between two people. Because we are not consciously aware of the factors that go into romantic attraction, we often end up frustrated and angry, not understanding why this person we love won't do what we want.

Romantic attraction is a very powerful force. However, even with all of its power and appeal, it should not be the only basis upon which to make a decision about a life partner. Romantic attraction is a start, but it should not be the only factor. The power of attraction certainly encourages us to spend time with another, learn about him/her, and interact with him/her. We need to do these things to see if the person behind the attraction is the person with whom we can develop a good relationship. The more completely couples understand why they were attracted to one another and how they can be beneficial to one another, the greater chance they have to translate the power of attraction into relationship satisfaction. Attraction may draw us together but it doesn't guarantee a happy ending.

WHAT WE WANT FROM A RELATIONSHIP...

We think that love and life should be easy; and if it isn't, most of us assume that something is wrong with us. Sadly, many people we work with feel like failures. They expend a lot of energy trying to make their relationship work but have about as much fun and success as trying to contend with a puzzle with half of the pieces missing.

Relationships are made up of many ingredients. Each person brings their own list of qualities, some from the past and some focused on the future. Trying to sort through those factors and put them in some order is difficult. Often the first thing we do is try to change our partner's agenda and convince him/her that our agenda is correct.

People learn how to relate to others, for better or worse, from their own families and other role models they experienced growing up. They will continue to interact with others in the same way, until they learn a new approach for relating. Most of us need a new set of instructions for viewing, building and maintaining a relationship.

People don't realize that they do, in fact, know some of the basic ways to make a relationship work. After all, most people usually have some successful relationships with friends and business associates, meeting individual and collective needs and goals. However, in our business relationships we do not usually focus on changing the other person when things go wrong. We look at what needs to be altered or clarified in our expectations and the expectations of our associates. We make sure that the job description is clear.

We believe that people will learn from the relationship models they experience. However, few of us are directly taught how to relate to another adult in a loving fashion which can lead to the kind of continual and mutual renewal we sense in those marriages we all wish we had. Many of us not only lack good role models for marriage in our families, but society also segregates us from the older generations. It might be in the stories that we hear from our grandparents that we can learn a model of marriage that survives crises and time.

While it makes people feel better to point to a possible cause of the hurt and anger they experience in their relationship, it really doesn't help much in the long run. They blame themselves, each other, or perhaps a third entity (which can range from the other man or woman, to a child, job, or the in-laws) focusing on the negative or what they don't want.

The first step in building a new relationship requires the individual to define what they **DO WANT** from their involvement with another instead of continually agonizing or complaining about what they do not have.

WHAT WE WANT FROM A RELATIONSHIP...

WE WANT IT TO BE USEFUL

Most people have the expectation that a romantic relationship will be useful to them. However, each person in a relationship will have a different idea about what that means. Some people think of usefulness as some material goods or object that they can get more easily or share with their partner. Other people think of usefulness as having an available companion to do things with or a warm body with whom to share space. Finally some people who are perceptive about themselves will find another person useful if they have personality traits and strengths from which they can benefit or grow.

If the relationship is to be useful to each partner, you will end up finding someone who is substantially different from you in many ways. It is in the differences that you find the strength and resources needed for a relationship. How couples view the differences and utilize the differences that each partner brings to the relationship is critical. It is important for couples to value the assets that each person contributes to the relationship and not be defensive about capabilities they don't have.

When romantic couples first meet, they often deny that there are differences, because they have been taught to look for others who share common interests, values, and backgrounds. Having things in common is important, but it is really the differences that bring the possibilities of growth. If people choose someone who has their same strengths and talents, then the relationship will not offer as much potential for growth to the individuals and could, quite possibly, become an arena for competition.

It is important for couples to understand and accept the differences between them. If the differences are not already recognized as a positive part of the relationship, they can easily become the topics that couples can blame as the cause of their problems. The differences present a more obvious target for people on which to focus, rather than the underlying emotional issues that may be the real cause of the pain and tension in the relationship.

If the differences are not acknowledged, then it is hard for either person in a relationship to feel truly accepted by the other. If the couple does not admit to its differences, it makes the whole relationship feel unreal. It doesn't feel safe when you or your partner is really one way but has to act another way.

Truly loving someone is accepting who they are. However, in order to really love another person you have to accept and love yourself. The real twist comes when you realize that you are very different from the person who is the object of your love and affection.

Tom thinks that Mary has changed over the years since they married and he would really like to have the Mary he married ten years ago. He thinks that she places too much emphasis on money and material things. He doesn't like the way she takes care of the house and feels that she is away from home too much. It is Mary's opinion that she has not changed but Tom has. She states that Tom was in favor of her having a career and expressed a desire to have equal responsibility for the children. She agrees that they have grown apart but she is not sure why. Bottom line, Tom and Mary don't enjoy being with each other as much as they used to.

Differences need to be viewed as strengths that can be utilized rather than weaknesses that can be destructive. For example, somebody who is outgoing and social may be paired with somebody who is shy and somewhat of a homebody.

These differences can be useful in a relationship because the couple, sharing the partner's individual strengths, can enjoy quality time at home and still develop an active social life with others beyond the home.

Relationships can be viewed as two different individuals bringing together their various talents and capabilities and pooling them, as would be done in a business setting. Thus both individuals are able to take advantage of each other's capabilities for their own growth and advancement.

As a relationship progresses, certain things begin to interfere with the couples' ability to pool resources. For one, the needs and skills of the individuals may change over time. A contribution needed at one point may begin to get in the way at a later time or even in a different place. The important thing is that each person in a relationship feels that they serve a purpose for the other in order for the relationship to effectively survive.

From counseling sessions, Tom and Mary realize that they have always been different and need to view these differences from another perspective. Tom realizes that Mary has always been a "higher achiever" than he is. He begins to understand that Mary's need to work is not a need to be away from him or the children. Mary comes to recognize that Tom is not as independent as she originally thought. She also learns that she can spend more time with Tom and the kids and not feel smothered. The importance of what they learn is that a need to achieve at work does not equate to a rejection of the partner and the need for more companionship does not equate with being consumed or controlled.

Sometimes, people decide to withhold or refuse to accept each other's assets because they feel hurt, cheated, or frustrated by the relationship in general. The net effect, of course, is that these couples no longer achieve their goals through cooperation. In fact, many begin to pull against each other, actually requiring more energy to accomplish anything.

Unfortunately, as the disappointments, frustrations, and hurts begin to pile up in a relationship, couples do tend to point to the very same differences that first drew them together. They end up blaming the basic ways in which they differ for the anger and dissatisfaction in their relationship. Over the years, these areas of conflict have even become a recognized legal reason for dissolving a marriage.

Some of the typical individual personality differences we find in couples are:

- realistic vs. idealistic
- optimistic vs. pessimistic
- trusting vs. suspicious
- dependent vs. independent
- shy vs. outgoing
- conservative vs. liberal
- quiet vs. talkative
- spontaneous vs. deliberate
- organized vs. scattered
- creative vs. concrete
- present focused vs. future focused

The impact of these individual differences can often be seen in conflict areas surrounding the following topics:
- Finances and how money is spent
- Sex and physical intimacy
- Communication styles
- Use of free time
- Personal interests and goals
- Openness to sharing each other and family time with friends and colleagues
- The meaning of emotional closeness

- Parenting styles and goals

Where do you and your partner stand on making the differences work for you?

- Can you quickly/easily list five ways in which you are different from your partner?

- Which, if any, of these differences makes your partner useful to you?

- What has changed about the usefulness of the relationship over time?

WHAT WE WANT FROM A RELATIONSHIP...

WE WANT TO BE ABLE TO TALK TO OUR PARTNER

In a romantic relationship most people want to be involved with somebody they can talk freely with about most anything, on both an emotional and intellectual level. A stimulating and creative conversation becomes a continual source of renewal for the relationship and an antidote to boredom. It is this kind of sharing that makes you want to turn off the television and just sit down and talk. Creative communication can make the individuals feel valued and special and allow each individual to experience the fun of contributing ideas and perspectives.

To engage in a stimulating and creative conversation requires more than good communication skills where he talks, she listens, she talks, he listens. The individuals must combine content or information with feeling. We have to go beyond a Dragnet style of communicating ("Just the facts") to include the facts and what we feel and think about those facts.

Looking back at Tom and Mary, we find that they engage in very little conversation. Mary feels as if she has lost her best friend and confidant. In the early years of their marriage, Mary described how she and Tom could talk for hours and never run out of things to say. Now they feel so tense around each other that they actually avoid communicating. Tom and Mary have begun to leave notes and voice mail messages for each other and exchange just the most basic information necessary to live with one another. Tom's point of view is that no one would want to talk with someone who is unpleasant to deal with. He feels that every time he says something that Mary does not agree with, she is determined to have a fight.

Many couples end up talking less and less and sharing as little as possible, literally and figuratively engaging in small talk. This basically means that the couple superficially reports the day's activities and trivia as content for conversation with no personal feeling or reaction. They stay away from any topic that might lead to a fight. You can spot these people at a fancy restaurant enduring the meal in silence because they have run out of things to say after discussing the weather.

It is easier to communicate with somebody with whom you feel safe. Many couples feel that they are able to talk to their partner in the first year or two they are together. Yet, as time goes on, many couples begin to feel less safe in sharing what they are thinking or feeling. This lack of safety usually develops over time when people feel that their partner no longer listens to them. Also, no matter what they say, they feel their partner points out that they are wrong. Finally, they have the sense that if they ever started talking they would not be able to stop, and would probably say things they would regret later.

Empathy, which many consider the gift of emotional connection, does not require that we completely replicate another's experiences. We have only to try to put ourselves in another's place, make comparisons to our own experiences, and bridge any gaps by trying to focus on what our partner is feeling.

It must be okay to disagree and agree to disagree. Couples have to be able to talk even if they don't see things the same way. (If you go back to the idea that we will be involved with people who are different, it should be a given that there will be differing perspectives or views on things.) When couples get focused on winning or losing the discussion, they in fact lose the ability to really hear their partner's perspective or reach a common understanding about the subject they are discussing.

When couples get caught up in believing that there has to be a right or wrong in a conversation, they usually end up in a power struggle and whoever knows the most can control the exchange of information. Or the couple simply never brings up the topics that can lead to disagreement, just to avoid the struggle. All conversations do not have to involve a winner or a loser to be meaningful. Actually, very few things are absolutely right or wrong.

When people can communicate clearly about what their needs are and how they would like them to be met, they won't engage in a hit and miss approach in attempting to support each other. To some extent, individuals who try to guess what would feel supportive to their partner almost always find themselves frustrated and/or in trouble. When people can communicate in a way where they understand where the other is coming from, it is easier to understand what they might need emotionally. This prevents the individuals from projecting their own needs and desires onto each other, in effect, giving their partner what they themselves would like to be given.

To make talking with each other feel more safe and comfortable, Tom and Mary develop a strategy to guide their communication. First they define the topics that have been off limits for them and try to determine why they have not been willing to talk about these subjects. They agree to develop a plan to handle these "hot topics". They talk about one topic at a time and stay in the present; not bringing up complaints from the past. They practice listening to what the other is saying and try to clarify what they hear. Finally, they try to be respectful of the other person's position when it differs from their own. This process takes Tom and Mary several months before they can report much real change. Rebuilding trust and respect will allow them to feel closer, and that takes time.

Where do you and your partner stand on being able to talk to each other?

- What subjects do you avoid talking about with your partner and why?

- Do you find that you pre-judge your partner's response to certain topics?

- What assumptions do you make about your partner before they even open their mouth?

- How often are you trying to <u>have </u>a conversation versus <u>win</u> a conversation?

- The last time you were upset about something, to whom did you talk?

WHAT WE WANT FROM A RELATIONSHIP...

WE WANT TO BE MUTUALLY INTERDEPENDENT; WE WANT TO BE CLOSE, YET SEPARATE

Simply defined, mutual interdependence is a state of being in a relationship that allows people to experience closeness while still remaining separate individual people. A precursor to mutual interdependence is the sense that who you are is worthwhile. You need to have a fairly clear idea of who one is as an independent person. If one doesn't, they will run the risk of becoming an extension of the other person, or a blank screen on which the other person chooses to see whatever they want to see. In mutual interdependence two individuals need to be able to coordinate their lives with each other without feeling smothered, controlled, or defined by the other.

Mutual interdependence seems to contradict the romantic concept of two people becoming one. It requires people to fight their own fears of loss by allowing somebody they dearly love to be free enough to leave the relationship. It also demands that people do not use the threat of leaving when they are upset with their partner. Actually, when mutual interdependence is in place, it allows people to be closer because they don't fear domination or devastation from potential loss of the relationship.

It feels better to be close with somebody who chooses to be with you because they like you rather than knowing they are with you because of fear or desperation.

Tom and Mary both report that they are basically living separate lives under the same roof. They have very little involvement with each other. When you ask either one of them why they are not more involved, they both state that they are trying to stay in the relationship and not be hurt. Neither Tom nor Mary wants a divorce. However, neither of them feels safe enough to allow a feeling of real need for the other. Tom states that in previous relationships he has found himself needing the other person too much and has promised himself that he would not do that with Mary. Mary reports always feeling alone, even as a child and thus finds her relationship with Tom no different from previous ones.

A true love is not kept around by fear or force. True love is best nurtured by people who feel they can be themselves. It is hard to be yourself when you have to worry that your partner would fall apart without you or that they might leave if they "really" knew you. Eventually people begin to resent giving up who they are to prevent loss. The best love that you can receive is the love that you can bear to lose.

As Tom and Mary learn to make use of their differences and communicate more openly, they begin to define how they really want to live as a couple. Tom realizes that he needs to be able to take chances in a relationship even if he gets hurt at times. He also has a clearer understanding of who he is and what he wants and doesn't fear being swallowed up by Mary. Mary also learns more about herself and makes the decision to be more involved with Tom than she has been with other important figures in her life. This means that she learns that falling in love with someone does not mean that she has to lose herself or her sense of independence. She learns that she can love Tom in a deep way and still be her own person. She learns to count on Tom, want things from him and still be okay if he doesn't come through.

Where do you and your partner stand on mutual interdependence?

- What are some ways in which you depend on your partner?

- How do you feel about this dependence?

- If you could no longer depend on your partner in these ways how would it alter your relationship?

- Do you feel that you are making a choice to be with your partner or are you afraid to be without him/her?

-If you feel afraid to be without your partner, how has that affected your ability to be close, open, and honest with him/her?

- Does it feel good to share most things with your partner, or do you feel that it is just easier to take care of things on your own?

WHAT WE WANT FROM A RELATIONSHIP...

WE WANT TO BE INVOLVED WITH SOMEBODY WHO RECOGNIZES US AS SPECIAL AND WHO IS SPECIAL TO US

A unique quality of human beings is their need to feel a sense of belonging. People often experience this need by being part of a family, belonging to a team, a club, a fraternity, or by becoming one of the "regulars" at a local establishment. What people get out of belonging is a sense that who they are is valuable and that they are noticed just for "showing up"; or simply that others in the group would notice if they were not present and are glad to see them when they are. This feeling of being valued is what we call "specialness". Therefore an important component in any relationship is feeling special to the other person in the relationship.

People's experience with feeling special and belonging is not the same, because of our divergent backgrounds. The individuals in a couple may differ greatly in what type of interaction makes them feel special. Couples need to keep in mind that just because one partner feels special when given gifts of flowers and candy and the other partner feels special when they are given a free afternoon alone does not necessarily reflect a difference in the love and commitment the couple may feel for each other.

It is a fairly basic human desire to feel that somebody sees us as special, unique, and valuable. Young children often get this feeling from their parents; yet, as the child becomes more independent and less compliant, it is difficult for many parents to continue to convey this message of specialness. One of the unique things that a romantic relationship can offer is a feeling of specialness that cannot easily be found elsewhere.

After ten years, Tom sees his importance to Mary as basically his wallet. He feels that his co-workers value him more than Mary does. At work people come to him to ask for help in solving problems. When he is away from work on vacation he feels that he is missed. Mary feels that Tom wants her to need him in ways that she doesn't need him. She states that if she doesn't make a big fuss over Tom when he comes home, he ignores her and basically treats her as if she is invisible. In actuality, Mary has no idea as to how she is special to Tom.

It is difficult to stay focused on the specialness of your partner when you feel angry or hurt by them. When the feeling of specialness is lacking in a relationship, most individuals report a real sense of loss or emptiness. It is not uncommon that individuals then look elsewhere for this feeling. When the real nurturing value of specialness is working in a relationship, anger and disappointment are easier to set aside. When you feel special and see your partner as special, you can feel proud and happy to be together.

Tom and Mary begin to talk and look at how they want to feel special to each other. Tom realizes that he wants to be seen as helpful and useful. Mary realizes that she just wants somebody to express satisfaction that she is there. Thus they both realize that their lack of feeling special has more to do with their own lack of clarity of what they individually require to feel special, than anything the other is or is not doing.

Where does your relationship stand in terms of providing a sense of specialness for you and your partner?

- What are some qualities or personal traits that attracted you to your mate in the beginning of your relationship? Do you still delight in them?

- What are some things about your partner that you now consider special and good for you?

- What does your partner value most about you?

- What do you wish that your partner valued about you?

WHAT WE WANT FROM A RELATIONSHIP...

WE WANT TO BE WITH SOMEBODY WHO LIKES US AND IS EXCITED ABOUT US

An important reason people want to be in a relationship is to have the experience that who they are and their very presence are enjoyed by another person. It simply feels good. We don't need to feel this all the time, because that would be unrealistic. However it would be hard to be supportive of or talkative with another person who we don't feel likes us very much or whom we don't personally like very much.

Mary and Tom both state that it is difficult for them to be enthusiastic or excited about being with the other. In fact, they find it uncomfortable to be in the same room for too long a period of time. Consequently, when they are at home together they tend to be in separate rooms or use the children as a buffer. They avoid each other because neither one believes the other one likes being around him/her. It is so bad, that Tom actually feels that the dog is happier to see him than Mary is.

Having a sense that somebody is enthusiastic about being with us makes us less sensitive to being hurt or offended by them. Conflict and disagreements are all part of dealing with a partner who is different from us. When you really enjoy your partner, you don't translate these differences and disagreements into disapproval and destructive criticism.

This concept is different from "public displays of affection" which are usually made more as a statement to others or as a way to reassure ourselves that we are really "in love".

In this area, Tom and Mary both have to work hard to break old habits. They have to consciously work at being more affectionate toward and appreciative of the other when they are together. This obviously does not feel natural at first. However, if Tom and Mary continue to work at being appreciative and caring of each other it will become habit, just as the negative reaction and avoidance became habit before.

Where do you and your partner stand on the expression of appreciation and caring?

- How often do you feel that your partner really enjoys your company?

- What is it that somebody can do or say that makes you feel that they want you to be around?

- How often do you simply look at your partner and feel glad that you are with them? If you don't, how do you let them know that?

WHAT WE WANT FROM A RELATIONSHIP...

WE WANT TO HAVE A PARTNER WHO RESPECTS US AND BELIEVES IN US

We need a partner who truly values our thoughts and ideas and accepts our basic character as a person. You do not want to feel that your partner wants you to be something different from whom you are.

When Tom and Mary first got married, they both felt that their relationship was helpful to them in dealing with their careers and stress. Now, they actually feel that their relationship is draining rather than strengthening. Both Tom and Mary feel that they have to work very hard to maintain peace when they are with each other. Also they find it difficult to be very honest with what they are feeling or thinking. Relationships feel draining and partners feel like unnecessary weight when the individuals do not give each other permission to be themselves.

For mutual respect to occur the following has to be present. To begin with, the individuals have to realistically see their partner. Romantic love, unfortunately, has the tendency to distort the perception of one's partner. Therefore, partners have to accurately see with whom they are involved, both the good points and the bad points. We have all heard the line about someone waking up one morning, rolling over in bed and wondering who they married. That is what we are talking about. Getting to know that person in bed with you is the first step.

Secondly, the individuals must accept who their partner actually is. This does not mean that we have to pretend to like everything about our partner. We simply allow them to be who they are so that our love is not given on a contingency basis, which requires the other to perform or change In order to continue receiving our love.

Accepting our partner differs from simply tolerating certain aspects of our partner's personality. Tolerance is a way of putting up with something you really don't like. The deep sighs, looking away, gritting the teeth, and stiffening the upper lip are all signs of tolerance, where you almost literally swallow the anger. No matter how much you intend to "keep quiet", there is usually a final straw that will at least momentarily break and make us "blow". These are the times we say, what we later wish we could take back. When true acceptance is present, we decide that the negatives are acceptable and the good outweighs the bad and we stop trying to change things that we don't like about the person.

The third requirement for mutual respect and belief in a relationship follows closely on the second. That is, the more we can accept our partner without trying to change him/her, the more open we will be to say what we really feel and think without fear of criticism and punishment.

Tom and Mary have to identify the things they do not particularly like about the other but will not change. Tom has to accept that Mary will never work on a project in the same way he does. She likes to work on several projects at one time, where Tom starts and finishes one project without taking a break. Mary has to accept that Tom will forever eat faster than she thinks is good for him. Once Tom and Mary stop trying to change the other, they can work on accepting the other (both the good and the bad) and focus more on a general sense of appreciation of who their partner really is.

Where do you and your partner stand on mutual respect?

- What is there about you for which you need more acceptance from your partner?

- What do you need to be more accepting of in your partner?

- What keeps you from being able to say whatever is on your mind to your partner?

WHAT WE WANT FROM A RELATIONSHIP...

WE WANT TO BE WITH SOMEONE WITH WHOM WE CAN FEEL SAFE TO BE OURSELVES

When we feel a sense of safety with our partner we can be ourselves without playing a role, walking on eggshells, or trying to be careful with the other. Safety allows us to "let our guard down" and behave in ways that are unfiltered and uncensored without fear of rejection or ridicule. It is easier to communicate with somebody with whom you feel safe. Safety is a fundamental building block of closeness and intimacy.

Neither Tom nor Mary feel like they can let their guard down and be themselves with one another. They report that it often feels like work to interact with one another. The tension is so great at home that their children are relieved when they do not have to deal with both of them together. Also, a once enjoyable sexual relationship is almost nonexistent.

When safety is present in a relationship, it actually takes less energy than if you have to hide or protect yourself in your interaction. When we "fall in love" we experience certain physiological symptoms when we are around the subject of our infatuation. These symptoms can include such things as heart palpitations, shortness of breath, sweaty palms, and lack of appetite. In looking at this list more closely it reads just like the symptoms of generalized anxiety or fear. If the symptoms don't subside as the relationship continues, one has to question why the fear (of loss) remains predominant. These early feelings of romance must be replaced with safety and the comfort of truly knowing one's partner.

The presence or absence of safety is most clearly demonstrated when there is a crisis. Couples can pretend there is safety on a day to day basis. However, when they actually have to work together dealing with a major problem, the lack of real safety can make that difficult. For example, in a relationship where there is little emotional safety between the adults, when a child gets hurt the parents may find themselves bickering with each other over the best way to deal with the injury rather than focusing on the child. When partners feel safe with each other they are able to admit to and express their vulnerability, both physically and emotionally.

This sense of emotional safety in a relationship is not the same as the safety and security people feel from simply being in a relationship, or in other words, having someone, anyone, to avoid the fear of being alone.

In order to put safety back in their marriage, Tom and Mary need to consciously work at being more emotionally honest with each other. They have to clarify what their expectations are of themselves and the other in terms of their relationship. They find that once safety has left a relationship, it takes time to return. Mary and Tom begin with small steps, trying to take risks in areas where they can afford to be emotionally vulnerable. With each step or risk received gently by the other they can begin to rebuild a sense of safety and trust.

Where do you and your partner stand on emotional safety?

- How often do you pretend that you are feeling something different than you really are when you are around your partner and just "playing it safe"?

- How often do you feel that your partner is "playing it safe" with you?

- What do you imagine your partner might need from you to feel safe? Can you check that out?

- What are some things that your partner could do that would allow you to feel safer in your relationship? Can you share your answers with your partner?

- Do you think there are any situations from your past that made you feel unsafe, which you are carrying over into your current relationship?

WHAT WE WANT FROM A RELATIONSHIP...

WE WANT TO BE WITH SOMEONE WHO WE BELIEVE WILL BE A PERMANENT PART OF OUR LIFE

Some of the expectations that we have in a relationship are the obvious big ones, for example, being with you until "death do us part". Some of the expectations are the smaller ones such as, listening to me when I have a problem, helping me with the children, and supporting me in my work. Permanence is a sense that you have a person in your life that you can count on to "be there" in definite ways. It makes you feel that they are there for you as a partner.

It is possible to have a life-time partner whose interactions leave you feeling alone most of the time. This happens because a real sense of partnership requires an intimate level of interaction beyond just living in the same house.

Divorce and death are simply two of the more obvious ways that permanence is challenged. There is no end to the ways that people can drain emotional energy and time away from their relationship. Without ever claiming a departure from the relationship, people find ways to focus and invest themselves elsewhere. Subtly but surely they leave their partner with a sense of abandonment. These emotional departures may involve the person committing an overabundance of energy to work, children, hobbies, or being with others in a way that excludes the partner.

Intimate interaction occurs only when people can share openly and honestly who they are and have a sense that the person they are sharing with is really interested in them.

One of Mary's biggest complaints about Tom is that "he is not there when he is there." She feels that Tom is always more interested in TV or his hobbies or the newspaper than in talking with her. Tom feels that it is impossible to be with Mary without the buffers of the TV or his hobbies. Tom states that without a buffer he becomes irritated and wants to lash out at Mary. She makes him feel that there is nothing he can do to help, so why bother listening.

Couples like Tom and Mary have to make a conscious choice to be more emotionally and intellectually present when they are together. Tom has to try to pay attention to Mary without dividing his attention with the TV, music, or the newspaper. Mary needs to make sure that she is receptive to Tom when he does respond or share, rather than assuming that he doesn't have anything of interest to say.

Where do you and your partner stand on permanence?

-Think about those aspects of your life that occupy a lot of your emotional and physical energy. Do some things get a bigger percentage of your time than others. Why?

- Assuming your partner has not made statements about leaving you, how much of the time do you feel alone in your relationship?

- Is there something in your partner's life with which you feel a sense of competition?

WHAT WE WANT FROM A RELATI

WE WANT TO BE WITH SOMEONE WIT
SHARE EXCLUSIVE ACTIVITIES AND _

In observing long term relationships, one can generally find a special activity or involvement that functions as a special bond for those individuals. This exclusive quality in a relationship goes beyond sexual monogamy or sharing practical aspects of marriage such as parenting or caring for a home. It is an exclusiveness that creates a strong and lasting connection that makes the relationship special to them and them alone.

Sadly, as the demands of married life and parenting increase, the special exclusive things we used to do are the first things to go. We hunker down under the stress and often stop talking, stop sharing, and stop working on projects together. The couple becomes functionally efficient, but it loses the sense of exclusivity that told them they were special to each other. Sometimes just taking the moment to share that exclusive experience can give both individuals the added energy to keep going.

When they first met, Tom and Mary enjoyed going to concerts and taking long hikes. Once the children arrived and their lifestyle changed, it seems the only common interest that Tom and Mary currently have are their children. When their kids went to spend a week with their grandparents, Tom and Mary didn't know what to do with each other, much less what to talk about. The two of them would say that they have just "grown apart". In actuality, what has happened to Tom and Mary is that they never worked on developing additional interests and activities beyond the ones they brought into the relationship.

Couples need to be adaptable to the changes that occur with age, physical capabilities, and changing interests so that they can develop new special and exclusive activities they can share. Exclusive activities do not have to be pleasurable. The couple might find it easier to do a certain job together, such as taking their dog to the vet for yearly shots, doing yard work, or doing the taxes together for that April 15th deadline. The job goes smoothly with the cooperation of two people and the couple can experience a sense of accomplishment in doing work with an enjoyable end result.

Tom and Mary make a conscious choice to put common interests and activities back into their relationship. To help with this, they establish a "date night" where they go out once a week without the kids. Also they plan mini-vacations once every three months when they go away for a long weekend without the children. These scheduled blocks of time allow Tom and Mary to have the "alone time" that is needed to rediscover or develop interests and activities that they can share.

Where do you and your partner stand on exclusivity?

- List five activities that you enjoy doing with your partner.

- List five topics that you enjoy talking about with your partner.

- When was the last time you and your partner spent a minimum of two days away from your children or other acquaintances, just the two of you?

- What happens that makes it difficult for you to spend the time you used to spend with your partner?

WHAT WE WANT FROM A RELATIONSHIP...

WE WANT EMOTIONAL SUPPORT

Most of us will say that the primary reason we want to be in a relationship is to have somebody who can provide us with help or comfort for our emotional or physical needs. Emotional support involves two individuals taking each other's needs into consideration and trying to be supportive and responsive to those needs.

Neither Tom nor Mary feel particularly cared for by the other. The void here may have been the most frustrating for them. They both say that they try to give the other what they think they want but it doesn't seem to make any difference. Mary feels that she has practically martyred herself to please Tom, but he doesn't appreciate it. Tom feels that trying to take care of Mary is like walking in a mine field. He reflects back, stating that if he makes the wrong step, she just explodes at him.

The area of emotional support in relationships has been confusing for couples, due to different theories about men's and women's emotional needs. It is our belief that men and women do have similar emotional needs. However, all individuals are unique. Men and women have to be responded to in specific ways which have been shaped by how they were raised as children.

The romantic ideal of emotional support is that "if you really love somebody you ought to be able to know what your partner needs when they need it". It would be very difficult to meet the expectations of this premise unless most of us were telepathic and could literally read minds. However, many people do in fact feel unloved when their partner cannot anticipate what they want.

Since most people are unable to read their partner's mind even though they love them, couples need to learn the following:

1. Each partner in a relationship needs to become aware of what the other personally needs and how that need can specifically be met.

2. The individuals need to be able to share their specific needs and the manner in which those needs can be addressed with their partner. Of course, safety is an issue here, because it is difficult to share what you need if you fear criticism or ridicule.

3. People need to be willing to work on addressing their partner's needs in a way that pleases their partner.

This issue of emotional support is very frustrating because most people are not aware of what they need, much less what their partner needs. Also, since we tend to become romantically involved with people who are different from us (given the usefulness of the differences) it is not easy for individuals in a relationship to automatically feel comfortable doing things their partner needs. Therefore, this area usually involves considerable work for any couple. It requires people to do a lot of self searching, and effective listening, to learn behaviors that may be unfamiliar to them.

When people do not find emotional support within their marriage, they will turn to other sources and friends, or they will try to deny their need in this area, cutting themselves off emotionally. Although friends are an important source of support, one's marital partner can be more readily accessible to give what is needed emotionally. We can't conveniently schedule times when we really need support. It happens when it happens, whether that is at three a.m. after a bad dream, or when we just feel upset for no apparent reason.

The area of emotional support will take the longest time for Tom and Mary to work on. The reason is that they both need to learn what they want from the other in terms of caring and support. Then they have to feel safe enough to share it with one another. Finally, there has to be a commitment to consciously make an effort to be present for the other in ways that they need. For Tom and Mary, believing that the other wants to "be there" emotionally is crucial to re-establishing the expectation of support.

Where do you and your partner stand on emotional support?

- How aware are you of what you need and want from your partner?

- How aware are you of what your partner needs and wants from you?

- How willing is either of you to change some of your behaviors to be more supportive of the other?

WHAT WE WANT FROM A RELATIONSHIP...

WE WANT IT TO BE USEFUL

WE WANT TO BE ABLE TO TALK TO OUR PARTNER

WE WANT TO BE MUTUALLY INTERDEPENDENT: WE WANT TO BE CLOSE, YET SEPARATE

WE WANT TO BE INVOLVED WITH SOMEBODY WHO RECOGNIZES US AS SPECIAL AND WHO IS SPECIAL TO US

WE WANT TO BE WITH SOMEBODY WHO LIKES US AND IS EXCITED ABOUT US

WE WANT TO HAVE A PARTNER WHO RESPECTS US AND BELIEVES IN US

WE WANT TO BE WITH SOMEONE WITH WHOM WE CAN FEEL SAFE TO BE OURSELVES

WE WANT TO BE WITH SOMEONE WHO WE BELIEVE WILL BE A PERMANENT PART OF OUR LIFE

WE WANT TO BE WITH SOMEONE WITH WHOM WE CAN SHARE EXCLUSIVE ACTIVITIES AND INTERESTS

WE WANT EMOTIONAL SUPPORT

We hope now that people have a clearer understanding of what to expect when they get involved with somebody else. Although we have discussed ten distinct expectations, we are aware that these expectations overlap. We encourage you and your partner to discuss the topics in this section and rank order the ten expectations in terms of what is most important.

These expectations are not the only answer to having a satisfactory relationship. Sometimes couples need to seek professional help to understand what may be causing difficulties in their relationship. However, after reading this section and answering the questions you may have more clarity about what is happening in your relationship than you had before. Remember, MAKING LOVE SAFE is not just a book that you read and put on the shelf, it is a blueprint for a process. This is a process of self awareness and sharing, so you can always know where you are and where you would like to go.

PART TWO

THE LANGUAGE OF LOVE

Often, what couples term difficulties in communication, are more than just an inability to talk to one another. In fact, some partners would say the problem is that their partner won't stop talking, nagging, or complaining; they just keep saying the same thing over and over again. For many couples it is not really a communication problem, but a listening problem.

Another "communication" problem is the way in which people try to express what they need from their partner. Some people assume that if their partner really loved them they would know what they wanted. Others try to express their wants indirectly through questions, or by doing for their partner what they really want done for themselves. They are actually hoping their partner will catch on.

It hurts when you don't get what you need or expect from your partner. It also hurts to not be able to please someone you love. When people feel hurt they will tend to withdraw in order to keep from being hurt again; or they will attack, so their partner will hurt the way they do.

Rarely have we seen individuals, particularly at the beginning of a relationship, intentionally refuse to give their partner what they want and need. People try to satisfy, but when their efforts don't work, they get frustrated. Some will keep trying with increasingly complicated efforts; they will even give up what they need in order to please their partner. Others just quit, assuming their partner can never be pleased.

People tend to be drawn to someone different from themselves, so it should not be surprising that these differences extend to how the individuals communicate and express their needs. Women tend to be more process oriented.

They pay attention to "how" something is done or how they feel. Men are more task oriented; setting the goal, solving the problem, identifying the behavior to be achieved. So we have a woman who says, "I don't feel loved", and the man will respond with "what more do you want me to do?". The woman is talking about "feeling". The man is talking about "doing".

Couples need to recognize that all individuals have feelings that can best be responded to with certain behaviors. A person's unique connection of feelings to certain behavioral responses is generally established when they are very young. Communicating with your partner requires that you first connect with your feelings in the hundreds of possible situations that are faced daily, then identify a behavioral response that would help you with that feeling, and finally communicate the whole equation to your partner.

Since couples have been continually frustrated with how to do this, we have come up with a plan that will provide the direction to meet the wants, desires, and differences of couples. There are sixteen strategies that can readily address the communication formula of:

"When I feel _____ I need you to do _____".

Underneath the adult complications, we have found that couples need to deal with feelings of hurt, fear and sadness, the same basic things children deal with. We still experience the same emotions whether we are young or old; we just need them addressed differently.

Being supportive of your partner in emotional times often requires setting aside judgment or evaluation. You may know that your partner is upset about a situation, but how your partner needs you to respond to his or her feeling about the situation is based upon **his or her** background, past experiences, and ability to receive— **not yours**. What would feel good to one partner will not necessarily feel good to the other.

People respond differently due to different previous experiences. Some people rely heavily on eye contact and what they see. Others rely on the substance and tone of what they hear. Some respond to touch and how people approach them physically. It is important for couples to understand the basic ways their partner responds and what they would need in different situations.

Beyond the external indicators and social signs of commitment, couples need to develop their own language of love and involvement. Most couples have, in fact, a private "short hand" in communicating. We encourage couples to go beyond the short hand and really work on and develop a common language of emotional support.

The sixteen strategy areas that follow have been developed for the purpose of giving couples the structures of that language. Each strategy is based on a feeling: those simple, uncomplicated feelings that we all began experiencing as children. Each strategy challenges the individual to identify what behavioral responses they need to each of the feelings. Most important, this information has to be shared with the partner. The goal is to provide information that can be used in future situations. This exchange of emotional information is not an attack or a vehicle for blame. Simply, individuals need to identify what they need and convey that information to their partner. In a loving relationship, your partner will be glad to know how he or she can support you more effectively.

We believe that individuals need to take personal responsibility for themselves as well as responsibility for the functioning of their relationship. We are not suggesting that individuals take responsibility for their partner. Part of assuming responsibility for oneself and the relationship is being able to identify what you want for yourself, as an individual, from the relationship and not blaming your partner for what you don't get and never request. The examples that we give in this book have been derived from some of the couples we have worked with over the years. We hope that they can stimulate your own self exploration in identifying what you want from a relationship.

We realize that sometimes your partner is unable or unwilling to give you exactly what you want in a given area. When this occurs, couples need to look at compromise in dealing with their personal requests. Unfortunately, romantic relationships often cause us to revert to childlike demands and behaviors. Too often if we don't get exactly what we want when we want it, nothing will satisfy us. Adult relationships require adult compromise, not childlike rigidity.

The myth exists, "If you really love me you would know exactly what I want and do it for me without me having to ask." A companion myth exists, "If I really love my partner, I would do exactly as he or she asks." Both are myths, and neither one is really possible. However, sometimes people expect too much of themselves and their partner. Compromise does not kill romance. It can actually enhance the long-term safety and trust of a relationship.

As you look at the following strategies with respect to how they can apply to you and your relationship, remember you are not embarking on a competition with your partner as to who does the most. The strategies should also not become the basis for a "tit for tat" exchange. If your partner does not show you recognition in the way that you want, that does not entitle you to withhold a response he or she might have requested. In a loving relationship there is an interest and concern for your partner's happiness. If that interest is gone and you are unwilling to be responsive to your partner, you need to address the lack of motivation directly rather than indirectly through withholding or withdrawal.

ASKING FOR PROTECTION

We all want to feel protected. In this area you are asked to think about and identify how you want your partner to protect you: to look at ways that you would want your significant other to be an ally. Second, you are asked to identify what you need from your partner when you are in a difficult or uncomfortable situation.

Protection does not cause one person to be dependent on the other, nor does it promote the fostering of a weakness, fear, or problem for the partner. When you feel protected by your partner you feel that there is someone working with you to try to prevent injury, harm, or discomfort from a particular person or situation.

Protection does not involve asking your partner to do something that would be part of the normal adult responsibility. For example, "I need you to call my boss and tell him I am running late". That would not be protection; that would be fostering dependency.

Protection is not about covering up a problem. For example, it would not be protective to make excuses to friends about why your partner seems to be sleepy all the time when he or she really has a drinking problem.

"I would feel protected ...."

"I would feel protected if you would sit down with me and go over all of our insurance policies and financial affairs. If something should happen to me, I want to know that you will have all of the information that you will need."

"It would be protective of me if you would quit slamming doors when something doesn't go your way. I am not saying that you cannot be upset, just try not to slam doors.

I startle easily and it takes me a while to calm down when I hear you banging doors."

"It would be protective of me if you would sit down and make out a budget with me so I can balance what we have with what we spend and how much we can reasonably save."

"It would be protective of me if you would go with me to the auto repair shop or the doctor or the IRS and just stay by my side. You don't have to say a word; just sit by me."

"It would be protective of me if you could try to let me know when you have had a bad day at work or are just in a bad mood."

"It would be protective of me if you could step in when you hear me losing my cool with our teenager. You can help calm things down without undermining me as a parent."

"It would be protective of me if you could run interference when we are at your mother's and she is being critical of us or our children."

Where do you and your partner stand on the strategy of protection?

- In what ways do you feel your partner is protective of you?

- In what ways are you protective of your partner?

- In what additional ways do you wish your partner were more protective of you?

- Are there situations when you wish your partner were a better ally?

- Can you think of situations when you know your partner would like some protection and you do not give it? Why?

- Are there ways that your partner tries to take care of you that make you uneasy or keep you dependent?

ASKING FOR RECOGNITION

With recognition, couples need to look at the ways each partner wants acknowledgment from the other. There are different levels of recognition. In the first level of recognition you are simply looking for another person to acknowledge your existence, by making a statement of greeting or acknowledging that you are there. Most people would probably say that this is a common courtesy that should always be there, even with total strangers.

The second level of recognition goes just a step beyond acknowledgment and involves asking someone how they are, what they have been doing or what they need. Most people experience this level of recognition whenever they do some type of business transaction. However, in business or social situations there is usually no expectation of a reply other than "fine." Since so many of our daily social interactions never go beyond the superficial recognition, it is important to have someone at home who is sincerely or genuinely interested in how we are or what we have been doing.

The third level of recognition is when somebody approaches you and asks about something that you have shared with that person from a previous conversation. Simply following up on past information can make people feel that they have been heard and are worthy of notice.

Recognition at the most intimate level is an acknowledgment and awareness of your partner's fears, hopes, and pain. This may include sensitivities about money, illness, work, family concerns, or spiritual issues. This type of recognition develops only after time and sharing openly with another person.

Recognition, particularly at the most intimate level, does not mean approval or even agreement on the topics that are shared. You may acknowledge that your partner has very strong feelings about the death penalty, abortion issues, etc., which you may not share. However, recognition allows for greater sensitivity to the individual when these topics arise in a couple's life.

Recognition or acknowledgment is not a difficult thing to accomplish if you know the areas in which your partner would like recognition. Acknowledgment can be conveyed by asking questions, making a simple verbal comment that you noticed something, or simply making eye contact and giving someone your full attention. Recognition is not necessarily conveyed by trying to fix something or solve a problem. Recognition is an acknowledgment, not a task to be done.

It is important for couples to have an understanding of when their partner does not need recognition or acknowledgment of something. For example, an obvious blemish on your partner's face, that you know he or she is uncomfortable with, does not need to be pointed out. Sometimes it is best not to state the obvious. Recognition is not a value statement. It is neither positive nor negative-simply an acknowledgment.

"I would feel more recognized if ...."

"I would feel more recognized if you called me by my first name rather than "honey" or "mom."

"I would feel more recognized if you could acknowledge what I do around the house and how I help with the kids."

"I would feel more recognized if you could acknowledge how important my religious life is to me."

"I would feel recognized by you if you could simply stop what you are doing and focus on what I am saying."

"I need you to recognize how strongly I feel about my students and their welfare. I would like it if you would ask questions about how my students are doing."

"I would feel more recognized if you said 'hello' when you came home from work."

"I would feel more recognized if you asked me how my day went and waited for the answer."

"I would feel more recognized if, when you came home, we followed up on the conversations we had in the morning about the day's activities."

Where do you and your partner stand on the strategy of recognition?

- What are some of the most important areas where you need your partner to show you recognition?

- How does your partner make you feel acknowledged?

- How can your partner let you know that he or she is interested in what you are saying?

- In what situations do you feel invisible to your partner?

ASKING FOR PRAISE

Most people need or want some sort of praise from their partner. We are defining praise as compliments or positive recognition of things that you do or your characteristics. Praise is an effective tool of parenting that helps children gain both a sense of competence and confidence in who they are and what they do. In adulthood we still need praise to continue to reinforce our sense of confidence and competence. As adults, the praise we receive comes in different forms than when we were children. We no longer get a gold star for a good homework assignment, but we might receive a performance bonus at the end of the year. Job advancement and employee recognition are types of positive acknowledgement we receive in our adult world. It may not be as direct as when we were kids, but praise still helps us feel valued.

Although most of us get some sort of praise for what we do at work, it will be our partner at home who can provide the most sincere praise in terms of who we are or those aspects of ourselves that we don't expose to our business world. Unlike children, who are dependent upon the praise parents and teachers choose to hand out, adults can actually ask for praise in the areas they need.

Rarely do people have an equal need for praise, and that is why it is important to know how much praise and what kind of praise your partner can handle. Praise is not necessarily a "quantity" issue, but more of a "quality" issue. Praise can be given in a "matter of fact" way, or it can be given with all the "bells and whistles". Praise can be given in private, in a public arena, or through "third party praise" (where you are complimenting your partner in conversation to another, with your partner listening). It is important to understand what types of compliments your partner is most comfortable with, as well as the frequency of them, and whether they need to be public or private.

"I would like more praise......"

"I need you to praise me about how I interact with our children. When you see me doing well, tell me."

"I would like praise for my projects around the house."

"I would like praise for something at least once a day, in addition to your comments about my cooking. I appreciate these compliments, but want more of other kinds as well."

"I would like compliments about my appearance when you think I look good. I need you to be specific about what you like. Don't just say 'you look nice'."

"I would like less praise. You praise everything I do, and I don't really trust that you mean it. It feels more like you just dole out praise because you are expected to do so."
"I would be most comfortable if you would praise me in private and not in front of other people."

Where do you and your partner stand on praise?

- What are important areas in which you need praise?

-Do you know what kind of praise your partner needs?

- Have you and your partner talked about your comfort level with the amount of praise and the way that praise is delivered?

- What types of praise make you extremely uncomfortable?

- In what areas do you wish you had received more praise as a child?

ASKING FOR DEPENDABILITY

To build a sense of trust and safety for children, it is important to follow through with what you tell them you will do. Parents know, all too well, that if you tell your child that they will get an ice cream cone after school, you need to get them an ice cream cone. The same premise holds true for adults. Adults also want promises to be kept, not because they are totally dependent on another for getting what they need (we can drive ourselves to the ice cream store) but simply because we need to know that we can count on others to keep their word.

Most people enter a romantic relationship with an expectation of being able to count on their partner. Earlier we looked at the broad expectations people have about relationships. Generally, the broad expectations cover the basics of honesty, fidelity, and companionship. However, it is also important to define what our dependencies are in a very specific day to day understanding. There are emotional foundations under these dependencies. Some of them are tied into longings that we have had since childhood, and that we have always wanted. Other explanations may simply have to do with the practicalities of living your life with another human being. It is useful to understand what those reasons might be. It is important, however, that you do not feel that you have to justify what you want to your partner.

"I need to be able to count on you to..."

"I need to be able to count on you to be home at the time you tell me. (It helps me to know your approximate arrival time so I can coordinate dinner and activities with the children)."

"I need to be able to count on you to be flexible as to when we can meet for dinner. (I have enough pressures on me at work right now without feeling that I have a deadline at home.)"

"It is important to me that we keep the promises we make to our children. (I am very sensitive to this issue due to the chaotic nature of my childhood.)"

"When we agree to a social commitment, I need to be able to count on you to follow through with it. I don't want you to stand me up. (It is embarrassing for me to have to explain your absence after I have already given our RSVP.)"

"I need to be able to count on you to tell me when you have issues with me."

"I need to be able to count on you to consult with me before you make purchases over $100.00."

Where do you stand with your partner with respect to what you can count on?

-What are the specific things for which you want to be able to count on your partner?

-What are the things for which you know your partner wants to be able to count on you?

-How comfortable are you requesting what you want from your partner?

-What are some of the things that you will have to rely on your partner for in order for you to be satisfied with the relationship (for example; fidelity, no physical abuse, no alcohol or drug abuse)?

ASKING YOUR PARTNER TO TELL YOU HOW YOU ARE BENEFICIAL

It is important for individuals in a relationship to hear on a regular basis how they are important to their partner. A fairly basic need that most of us have is to feel that certain aspects of who we are really have a positive impact on others, particularly a loved one. Feeling that we are beneficial helps support a sense of positive self-esteem and feelings of competence.

For many of us, our childhood plays a large role in determining the unique ways we want to make a difference to others when we are adults. Often the way we want to be beneficial grows out of those areas in which we experienced frustration as a child. It may stem from a personal quality that was not appreciated or recognized in the family: our sensitivity, competence, intelligence, loyalty, reliability or family commitment. If one comes from a family situation that is chaotic, it is not unusual to look for a romantic partner who needs our help and guidance. If one is the youngest in a family with lots of brothers and sisters, they will often look for a partner that they can educate or teach or lead.

If the desired area of impact is not acknowledged by one's partner, the tendency is for the person to seek acknowledgment elsewhere. The acknowledgment might come from another person, the workplace or even the children. The important thing to note here is that whoever or whatever acknowledges this important area of impact for the individual may gain greater importance than a partner who does not.

When we talk about someone benefiting from his or her partner we are talking specifically about how certain actions or words can be helpful or of value to the person. This involves the partner reflecting on the level of benefit provided by the other and telling his or her partner about the positive impact.

76

We may, in fact, be beneficial to our partner, but we also need to hear about it.

"I need to know that you find it beneficial."

"I need to know that you find it beneficial when I listen to you talk about your work."

"I need to know that my sensitivity to your sexual needs is not only pleasurable but means something to you in terms of how I value and respect you."

"I need to know that you benefit from my sense of humor."

"I need to know, when you ask for advice, that I say something useful or beneficial to you."

"I need you to say that you appreciate and benefit from the effort I put into my work, taking care of the kids, caring for our parents, etc."

Where do you and your partner stand on being beneficial to each other?

- What is there about you that you need to hear your partner say that he or she appreciates?

- What do you think your partner needs to hear you say that you appreciate about him or her?

- Can you identify the personal benefits you receive from your partner?

- Have you ever found yourself drawn to a person, other than your partner, or activity because you felt more appreciated?

ASKING FOR ACCEPTANCE

We all need to feel accepted for "who we are." All of us have some aspects of ourselves that are deeply ingrained and are not going to change over time— physical, mental, social, and emotional characteristics that make each of us unique. Our basic likes and dislikes and how we express ourselves don't change easily. In addressing the issues of acceptance we need to view these inherent tendencies as different from habits such as smoking, overeating, sloppiness, or tardiness that could be changed with some concentrated effort.

It is important that we feel that the person we are with is not trying to change these most basic personality characteristics, or just tolerating them. We need to feel a sense of acceptance for who we are. If we don't feel this acceptance, then these characteristics can often become exaggerated out of frustration. For example a person's need for order and cleanliness can become exaggerated by a partner's jokes about those particular traits.

When we feel a sense of acceptance, we are able to let our guard down and be more vulnerable with our partner. When we feel that somebody is not trying to change us, we are more willing to try to accept who that person is. Acceptance is not something that people normally get in the everyday world, because employers and teachers do not feel that they have to accept who we are. Rather, in many of the situations we deal with in society, someone is trying to mold us in one way or another. This intensifies the need to find acceptance at home.

Mutual acceptance, as well as self acceptance, is a must for couples in order to be truly accepting of their own children. Too often we put our children down for things we feel criticized for by our partners or things we dislike about ourselves.

We tend to be drawn to someone who is clearly different from us in many personality traits. The reasons for this are many, but the differences create both excitement and tension.

It is interesting that even though we are drawn romantically to someone who is different from us, we secretly harbor the belief that if we work at it long enough we can make our partner be like ourselves. The back side twist of this relationship pretzel is that if our partner does accommodate and change to become more like we are, we may lose interest in him or her because we were drawn to the differences in the first place. Accepting another for who they are means that we have to be secure enough with ourselves so that we don't need to replicate who we are in our partner for reassurance and reinforcement.

"I need you to accept ...."

"I need you to accept how I express myself emotionally. Please don't laugh at me when I cry."

"I need you to accept the fact that at times I question myself about my work situation. I don't need you to be critical or anxious when I talk about my concerns and doubts."

"I don't need you to make fun of me because I worry about having enough money to meet our expenses, even if you don't agree. I need you to accept that I do have fears about financial security because of my experiences as a child."

"I need you to accept that I have my own little eccentric areas. Please don't tease me about my fear of heights."

"I need you to accept that I tend to see things as 'black or white' and have difficulty seeing the gray immediately."

"I need you to accept that I will look in on my mother once a week."

"I need you to accept that I do the best I can."

Where do you and your partner stand on acceptance?

- What is there about you that you need your partner to be accepting of?

-What is there about your partner that you have been trying to change but now need to accept?

- If your partner has tried to accommodate to changes that you have requested, has that made him or her more attractive to you?

ASKING FOR HONESTY

Most people would say that they expect their partner to be open and honest. People don't consciously plan to have a relationship with someone who lies to them on a regular basis. Asking for honesty does not imply that your partner is lying. It is simply addressing the common concern in relationships that partners be open and forthright and not withhold what they are feeling or thinking.

It is important to be honest with your partner in a way that is caring but not harmful. Thus there is no need for couples to share every fantasy or dream with their partners that might injure or distress them. Direct honesty can sometimes be used as a weapon. Often the motivation for "bluntness" or "directness" is really to punish or to hurt.

Sometimes people feel the need to "confess" certain things they have done in the past, more to alleviate their own guilt or to punish their partner than to be open and honest. When we are caring about someone, we might omit something that would be unnecessarily hurtful and does not have a clear benefit or reason to be said. For example, it may not be caring to share with your spouse how attractive you found another person at a party.

There is a difference between caring for somebody and being careful with somebody. When you are being less than honest, with the motive of being "careful", you are really being self-protective because you feel that your partner cannot handle what you have to say. Being careful and withholding information usually breeds fear and anxiety on both partners' parts. Most people know when someone is handling them in a "careful" rather than "caring" manner.

"I need you to be more honest and open about..."

83

"I need you to be more honest about what you are feeling when we are together. The look on your face speaks loudly. If you feel angry, please tell me. I can take it. Or, if you are bored or distracted, let's discuss it."

"I need you to be honest and clear about what you want to do on the weekends with our friends. It is not fun to be with you knowing that you are miserable about doing something."

"I need you to be more honest with me about what you like and dislike sexually."

"I would like some suggestions about what you would like for your birthday. I don't like to play the game of guessing what you want."

Where do you and your partner stand on honesty?

-What are some of the things that you have failed to share with your spouse because you didn't trust how he or she would react?

- Are there situations when you feel your spouse may be withholding information or feelings from you?

- Are there some situations when you have justified dishonesty out of caring, when you were really being careful?

ASKING YOUR PARTNER TO PLAY

Early in a relationship a couple is usually able to have its own fun, or engage in what we call "free play". "Free play" involves being able to do fun things and interact in a playful spontaneous fashion without using alcohol, toys, or other people. The ability to play allows for laughter and interaction and also reduces tension and frustration.

For many couples it becomes more difficult to play as their relationship goes on. Time pressures, responsibilities and family demands consume the free time needed for play. Or, as they mature, partners may feel that play is not appropriate "adult" behavior.

Sometimes couples need to understand the types of play that are okay with their partner. For example, some people really enjoy teasing and sarcasm, while others find it irritating. It is important for the couple to talk about the type of play that each is comfortable with, rather than making the assumption that just because one partner likes to tease, the other should like to be teased.

Sometimes it feels safer to play with one's partner when alcohol is involved or when other people are around. This may reflect a tension level that exists on an on-going basis with the partner. Being able to engage in free play also seems to be an effective stimulator of sexual activity between individuals. The more partners can play, the more safety there is. The more ability to be receptive and vulnerable to one's partner, the more sex there is.

Couples often find themselves becoming competitive in situations that began as "play". Healthy competition is appropriate in many activities. However, when competitiveness or "winning" becomes the goal, the value of spontaneous playful interaction is lost.

"It would be easier for me to play if..."

"It would be easier for me if you would initiate more play, so that I don't feel like it is all my responsibility to make sure we have fun together."

"It would be easier for me to play if when we start having fun and laughing we can get back to what we are supposed to be doing and get serious without you getting mad or feeling abandoned."

"If would be easier for me to be playful if you would be sensitive to when it is a time to play and when it is a time to be serious. Ask me if you are not sure."

"It would be easier to be playful if we could spend some time together focused on us rather than just the daily tasks."

"It would be easier for me to play if you don't have too much to drink when we are out."

"When we are with friends, it would be more comfortable for me if I felt that it is okay to cut up with them as well as with you."

"I wish we could play and have fun together, without always needing other people around."

"It doesn't feel like play when you make fun of other people."

Where do you and your partner stand on Free Play?

- Do you feel that there is enough play between you and your partner?

- What are the barriers that keep you from playing more freely with your partner?

- Who in the relationship has the greatest control over how much you play?

ASKING FOR REASSURANCE
AND ENCOURAGEMENT

Most people bring some insecurities or weak areas into their relationships. It is natural to look to our romantic partner to tell us that we are okay. No matter how old or successful we are, most of us have a need for reassurance and encouragement from those that we trust.

It is normal and acceptable for children to look to their parents for support when they feel anxious, afraid, or confused. Sometimes, however, children lose the ability to ask for reassurance or encouragement due to repeated frustration or punishment. Others are raised with the notion that once we are adults we should not need reassurance or encouragement. Yet it is normal and acceptable for adults to look to their partner for appropriate encouragement and reassurance.

Although both responses are supportive, reassurance and encouragement are different. Reassurance occurs when a person is looking for an opinion as to whether an action or position is a reasonable one. Reassurance is only possible when someone has enough information to be knowledgeable to offer an opinion. People can not really offer an opinion or be reassuring in an area where they know nothing. Trying to reassure someone about something you know nothing about often comes across as a put down or as taking the person's position too lightly. No one wants to be reassured about the chances of obtaining a certain type of job when the partner has no idea whether it is possible or not.

When your partner comes to you with a problem or an issue that you cannot reassure them about, you can encourage your partner to pursue that issue or seek someone who is more knowledgeable and could reassure them about the situation.

Encouragement is the ability to stimulate or inspire someone to keep going. Encouragement can be just as useful as reassurance at times. It is an effective way to inspire partners to do something when we cannot guarantee the outcome. We may not know exactly what they are pursuing or be able to "walk the path" with them, but we can cheer them on. No one can guarantee the outcome of a football game; however, the cheerleaders do their best to encourage the crowds and the team to stay with the effort until the end.

"I would feel more encouraged/ reassured if you would..."

"I need you to encourage me to pursue this promotion at work and reassure me that you won't leave if I don't get it."

"When you hear me speak to a customer on the phone, I need you to reassure me with a "thumbs up" that I am speaking calmly and clearly."

"I need reassurance that you are okay with us having less money, if I go back to school."

"I need reassurance that you still find me attractive at age forty."

"Encourage me to stick to my diet."

"Occasionally reassure me that I am still a good lover."

Where do you and your partner stand on encouragement and reassurance?

- What are some things about which you need reassurance from your partner?

- In what areas have you not asked for reassurance and why not?

- What are some of the areas where you have sought reassurance when you really needed encouragement?

ASKING FOR EMOTIONAL ANCHORING

Emotional anchoring is best described as when individuals go to another individual because they are upset, angry, or confused and ask for a type of support or a specific behavior that will help them feel calmer and in more control of their emotions. It is a very natural human response to seek support when we are upset. When we were children we, hopefully, were able to turn to our parents when we felt on the brink of "losing control". We felt confident that our parents would calm us and help us return to a sense of balance. Sadly, for many adults, there is no one with whom they feel safe enough to express their emotions, other than a therapist or a member of the clergy.

Emotional anchoring differs for people depending upon how they were raised. Some individuals need time alone before they are willing to share their emotions with their partner. Others feel compelled to share their emotions and feelings immediately. Sometimes people just need somebody to listen to what they have to say or simply to let them ventilate, without any feedback. Some people want some critical evaluation of where they are coming from or even solutions. Some people don't want to have to say anything at all, but simply want to be held.

People need different things from their partners when the issue they are upset about is directly related to their relationship, as opposed to when the issue has nothing to do with their relationship. Couples need to be clear with how to "step through" an argument or disagreement inside the relationship. When the issue is within the couple, the stakes are higher than when it's an outside issue. When one member of the couple is upset with the other, the partner is needed to provide an arena of safety for an expression of feelings. This can be difficult for partners, because they are emotionally involved with the issue and sometimes the source of the distress.

"When I am upset, angry, or anxious I need you to...."

"When I am angry, scared, or confused I need you to just hold me for a while."

"When I am upset about something at work, I need you to listen to me rant and rave and say nothing at all. I would be interested in your comments once I have calmed down enough to listen to them."

"When you see that I am upset about something, please leave me alone until I ask you for your help."

"When I am upset about something that has happened to our children at school or in the neighborhood, I need you to respond to me and the situation objectively and help me gain a better perspective of what we can do to respond."

"When I am angry with you, I need you to listen and not argue with my feelings, as long as I am not being abusive."

"When I am angry with you, give me time to cool off before we talk. I will let you know about how much time I need so you are not left 'hanging'."

Where do you and your partner stand in terms of Emotional Anchoring?

- What do you need from your partner when you are upset about something outside the relationship?

- What do you need from your partner when you are upset with them?

- What specific things are you supposed to do for your partner when he or she is upset with you or something or someone else? How do you feel about what your partner needs from you?

ASKING FOR CONSTRUCTIVE PUSHES

A benefit of having a close relationship is being able to ask your partner for a "constructive push" concerning a particular topic or situation. A constructive push is defined as a gentle "nudging" or "nagging" to get partners to do something about which they tend to procrastinate.

A critical and defining aspect of constructive pushes is that the partner who recognizes the need for a nudge has to request it. One partner is not allowed to decide for the other partner the areas in which he or she should have constructive pushes. This strategy requires a truly trusting relationship because you are allowing your partner a "limited license" to nag you about a situation that may be fearful or uncomfortable for you.

A tricky aspect of constructive pushes is how closely they come to asking your partner to "parent" you. When you ask for a constructive push, you need to be specific about the area in which you want to be pushed and offer very specific instructions about how far you are willing to let your partner push you. In asking for a "constructive push", you are not turning over responsibility for your behavior to your partner; you are asking for help from someone whom you trust and with whom you feel safe.

One of the reasons for seeking constructive pushes is that if you request help in remembering something, you will be less defensive about the reminders. Also you will be less likely to "kill the messenger" when you requested the message in the first place.

"I need you to give me a constructive push......"

"I need you to push me to make a dental appointment to have my teeth checked. Just remind me that I only have to clean the teeth I want to keep."

"I need you to remind me to start working on the taxes before mid-March. Tell me we can go out and have a nice dinner when I am done."

"I need you to give me a push to winterize our cars before the first snow. Ask me about once a week if I have taken care of this, starting on or about November 1st."

"I need you to tell me when you see me berating myself or failing to accept a compliment from others. Please do it privately and don't make a big deal of this in front of others."

"I need you to remind me to start working on my report at least a week before my deadline. Ask me if I'm aware of the time until the deadline. I'll respond without being defensive."

"As I am trying to change my eating habits, if you see me reach for a "forbidden" food, ask me if I am aware of what I am doing. Sometimes I may just reach for the cookies without even thinking."

Where do you and your partner stand on Constructive Pushes?

- What are those situations or topics requiring a push from your partner and how can he or she push you?

- What areas or topics are off limits in terms of constructive pushes?

- Do you feel you and your partner equally ask each other for constructive pushes?

- If it does not feel safe to ask your partner for a constructive push, why, why not?

ASKING FOR ALLOWANCE FOR MISTAKES

All of us have certain habits or behaviors that we would like to change. Sometimes our motivation is internal and sometimes the changes are initiated through the urging of family members. People working on change need to know that their partner will not come down on them every time they have a slip up or do not follow through in the way in which they would like. People need to have freedom and feel a sense of safety to make mistakes.

As in the strategy for constructive pushes, it is important that a partner ask specifically for the areas in which he or she would like some "allowance for mistakes". When the individual identifies the areas where he or she will consciously work for change, responsibility for the behavior will stay where it belongs and will not promote a parent-child interaction between the couple. For many adults, the more slack they have, the less likely they are to rebel. Change can therefore occur more quickly, because it does not get caught up in a power struggle or rebelliousness.

There are certain habits or behaviors that obviously cannot be given a great amount of slack by one's partner. Physical or emotional abuse, infidelity, alcohol or substance abuse, and reckless driving are areas where a spouse may feel compelled to lay down limits that cannot be violated.

"I need you to give me some allowance for mistakes when...."

"I need you to allow for my mistakes when I am doing a repair project around the house to save us money. If it doesn't work out just right, please be flexible and forgiving."

"I need you to give me a break if am occasionally late."

100

"I need you to refrain from joking with our friends about what I wear. I am working on improving my wardrobe and don't need to be kidded about it."

"If you see me doing something you think is stupid, I need you to ask me about it before you jump to a conclusion and assume I am making some mistake."

"I say or do something that hurts your feelings. We need to talk about it to be sure I understand how this happens and how it affects you. If you start with the assumption that I meant to hurt you, it will only miss the point that I need to become more sensitive to your feelings."

"I am willing to change my attitude and the way I do some things in the interest of improving our relationship. However, I need you to allow me some slip-ups in my efforts along the way. I cannot change overnight those habits I have built up over many years."

Where do you and your partner stand on Allowances for Mistakes?

- What are some behaviors that you are trying to change and about which you need some slack from your partner?

- What does your partner do that makes it difficult to make certain changes or makes you not want to change certain behaviors?

- What is it you do to encourage your partner to change certain behaviors?

- What do you do to discourage change in your partner?

- Are there things that you do to spite or upset your partner?

ASKING FOR EMOTIONAL REPLENISHMENT

When an individual is feeling emotionally or physically drained, depleted, or worn out, he or she needs to be replenished. It is often easier to identify how we need to be physically recharged, but there is also an emotional component to replenishment. People will respond to different types of replenishment or nurturing depending upon what they experienced growing up. Some people can actually be replenished by simply being left alone when they are emotionally or physically drained or physically ill. Some people can be recharged by being distracted from their physical or emotional state, by being taken to dinner or a movie. Finally, there are those people who need to be pampered to feel replenished.

Partners have to be comfortable with their partner needing something different from what they need. There is nothing worse for someone who needs to be left alone than to have his or her concerned partner hovering around. Likewise, the person who likes to be pampered should not feel hurt or rejected when his or her partner does not want pampering.

The extrovert/ introvert factor affects the individual approach for replenishment. Extroverts are generally replenished or charged up by activity or spending time with others. Introverts refuel by having time alone.

"When I am drained or under the weather, I would like you to...."

"When I am feeling drained I need you to listen to me just talk about the things that are going on in my life."

"When I am out of energy, I need you to think of a special activity that will take me away from it all (dinner, a movie, parents' Saturday alone)."

"When I come in and am worn out at the end of the day, just let me watch TV and not have to talk for a while. Give me time to unwind, then come sit with me."

"When I have had a hard week and need to recoup over the weekend, it helps when you take care of the children on Saturday morning and let me sleep late without interruption."

"When I am sick, I need you to bring me foods that I like and massage my back and neck."

Where do you and your partner stand on Emotional Replenishment?

- What is the best way your partner can help you recharge when you are feeling drained?

- What is the best way to recharge your partner when he or she is feeling drained?

- How are you and your partner different in the area of emotional replenishment, even in terms of what you need when you are sick? What difficulties or compromises do these differences require?

ASKING FOR VERBAL AFFECTION

Couples need a vehicle to express their affection and caring in ways other than physically and/ or sexually. Verbal affection is a unique and special form of positive recognition, most comfortably found within the boundaries of a romantic involvement.

Beyond the external commitments of love and marriage vows, it is important for people to hear verbal statements of love and appreciation and caring which their partner has for them. Most people need reassurance that their partner wants to be with them and they need to hear it in a way that makes them "feel" loved and cherished.

It would be unusual for people to have a romantic relationship without accompanying statements of verbal affection. In fact, statements of verbal affection are often a necessary precursor to physical affection. Interestingly, the whole area of verbal affection may seem like such a basic component of a relationship that it resists much explanation. However, sadly, many couples drift away from the statements of affection that helped define their early romance.

Couples need to learn not only how to express those statements that their partner would be comfortable hearing, but also how these statements should be made. Often, individuals are more comfortable getting and receiving verbal affection if they received it as a child. Whether someone is comfortable receiving verbal affection in private rather than in front of others is also a variable that reflects past history.

It is important not to pull for a verbal response from your partner every time you make one. The expression," I love you", should not become a command for an "I love you, too" in response. When this kind of responsive pressure is felt, the couple has left the realm of expressing verbal caring and moved into the arena of manipulation and control.

"I would feel more cared for if you could...."

"I would feel more cared for if you could say 'I love you' at least once a week."

"When you tell me that I am your 'teddy bear', I really feel special to you."

"I would feel more cared for if you could let me know that you are glad to see me, when I come home at night."

"I would feel more cared for if you used my real name and forget that nickname you've been using. I feel more grown up and accepted that way."

"'I wish you would say 'Hullo, Darlin', more often. It makes my heart flutter."

"You say 'I love you' so often, it really makes me wonder what you want. It would mean more to me if you just told me you loved me at special times."

Where do you and your partner stand on Verbal Affection?

- What affectionate statements do you really like to hear from your partner?

- What affectionate statements do you feel your partner wants to hear? How do you know?

- Do you feel that there is too little, too much, or just enough statement of verbal affection in your relationship?

- Do you ever feel manipulated by your partner's statements of verbal affection?

ASKING FOR PHYSICAL AFFECTION

In adulthood most people look for fulfillment of their need for physical affection within a romantic relationship. Physical affection covers the full continuum of non-sexual to sexual contact: light touches, caresses, holding, playful physical contact, hugs, sexual touching, kissing, sensual stroking, and intercourse.

Everyone has had different experiences with physical affection in childhood. Consequently a couple needs to be clear about what types of physical contact and affection are needed, when and where it can be expressed, its frequency, and the types of physical contact that are "off limits" or unacceptable.

Couples need to develop a mutual understanding about what kind of contact feels playful and enjoyable in a non-sexual way and what contact feels sexual. People differ greatly in terms of what is sexual versus non-sexual. Partners should not assume that what a gesture means to them means the same thing for their partner. It is also important for couples to be aware of and talk about the precursors of sexual affection, time, and circumstance that will allow for comfortable and optimal sexual involvement.

There seem to be three circumstances that need to be present for a couple to have a long term satisfying sexual involvement. First the couple needs to feel safe to play and laugh and "cut up" with one another. Secondly, couples need to feel that they can be honest about what they want and need from the other in all emotional areas, not just the sexual area. Finally, couples need to be able to disagree and potentially fight with one another in non-destructive ways. When present, these factors can be the foundation of a strong sense of trust and safety with a partner. It is this sense of trust that allows couples to be sexually receptive over a sustained period of time.

"I would feel physically cared for if you would..."

"I would like you to hug me when I ask, without your expecting it to be an invitation for sex. Sometimes I just want to be affectionate."

"I like holding hands with you when we walk. It makes me feel connected."

"I would like you to just hold me before we go to sleep or after we have made love."

"When I am washing dishes, please don't come from behind and grab me. It feels more like a sneak attack than affection."

"Please don't drape yourself over me when we are with friends. I am not comfortable with public displays of affection."

"Please know that even though I do not have as strong a need to be as sexual as you, that it does not mean that I care for you any less."

Where do you and your partner stand on Physical Affection?

- What types of physical affection needs have you not shared with your spouse?

- Do you feel that you provide your partner with enough physical affection?

- Have you and your partner ever talked about what is **not comfortable** for you in your sexual relationship?

-Do you ever feel that your partner is "crowding" you in the way he or she touches you?

ASKING FOR FORGIVENESS

For couples to continue to grow closer, they have to be willing to let go of hurts and resentments that are stored up from the past. If partners can ask for forgiveness from one another, it allows them to continue moving forward in their relationship and not become bogged down with hurt and anger.

When an individual makes a request for their partner to forgive them, they are not assuming total responsibility for their partner's hurt, nor are they stating that they did anything deliberately. The request for forgiveness is a statement that individuals are aware that they have done something that has deeply hurt their partner and they are sorry that the hurt has occurred.

Sometimes the wrongdoing is an obviously damaging act, such as infidelity, financial indiscretions, or abusive behavior. More often than not, however, we have unknowingly hurt the one we love, either through a misunderstanding or because we are in a confused emotional place.

There is a difference between (1) seeking forgiveness to feel better and (2) seeking forgiveness for the sake of healing a relationship. When we seek forgiveness to feel better we usually are doing it to manipulate our partner or perhaps even to punish or blame him or her. For example, a desire to unburden one's guilt by talking about a sexual indiscretion that happened a long time ago can cause more damage than good.

When individuals ask for forgiveness from their partner without making any commitment to change their behavior, the act is hollow. If you find yourself continuing to ask forgiveness for the same problem over and over again, you need to look at your own commitment to your partner and willingness to change.

Long-standing romantic commitments have three aspects. There should be (1) commitment to the partner, (2) commitment to the relationship, and (3) commitment to self. Asking for forgiveness supports and strengthens all areas of commitment. We should ask our partner's forgiveness because we are committed to him or her. We also seek forgiveness because we are committed to the relationship, and do not want it to be damaged. Finally, we need to take responsibility for our actions, which requires forgiveness because of a commitment to ourselves to be honest. It is hard to have self-respect when we know we have hurt someone we care about and don't take responsibility for what we have done.

It is also important that we be able to forgive ourselves for what we have done to our partner. Often there can be a huge barrier between two people when one of the people is full of self hatred. The forgiving process is complete only when offended persons have forgiven, and the offender has forgiven himself or herself.

Couples should also share those areas or situations in which they would hope their partner would seek forgiveness from them. It is possible for people to hurt someone they love and not be aware of the significance of the hurt. If couples can share the hurts that are not talked about or recognized by the offending partner, then resentments and grudges do not have a chance to grow. This aspect in the forgiveness process needs to be viewed as the information exchange, which is important to one's commitment to the relationship.

"I wish you could forgive me for..."

"I wish you could forgive me for not being more accepting of your parents when I first met them."

"I wish you could forgive me for not backing you up when you disciplined the children."

"I wish you could forgive me for making statements to our friends that should have been kept private."

"I wish you would want forgiveness for..."

"I wish you would want forgiveness for forgetting my birthday."

"I wish you would want forgiveness for the many times you have raised your voice and belittled me."

"I do not hold it against you that we don't have a lot of extra money. It would help our relationship if you could forgive yourself for not making as much money as you had hoped."

Where do you and your partner stand on Forgiveness?

- Identify different situations or actions in which you have been involved that you know hurt your partner and for which you would like forgiveness.

- Would your partner state these same events on their list of ways they have been hurt, or would their list be different and how?

- What has your partner done to you that you wish he or she would want forgiveness?

- For what do you need to forgive yourself because it is interfering with your relationship?

ASKING FOR....

PROTECTION

RECOGNITION

PRAISE

DEPENDABILITY

YOUR PARTNER TO TELL YOU HOW YOU ARE
BENEFICIAL

ACCEPTANCE

HONESTY

YOUR PARTNER TO PLAY

REASSURANCE AND ENCOURAGEMENT

EMOTIONAL ANCHORING

CONSTRUCTIVE PUSHES

ALLOWANCE FOR MISTAKES

EMOTIONAL REPLENISHMENT

VERBAL AFFECTION

PHYSICAL AFFECTION

FORGIVENESS

We have attempted to clarify how partners can communicate with each other emotionally. By following the sixteen different strategies you should be able to have a common language to help mediate the differences that will exist in any romantic relationship. Please keep in mind that in each area a given individual may have more requests than the other. Requests do not have to be matched equally. Some requests your partner might have could be impossible for you to accommodate for numerous reasons, whether emotional or physical. Many of the strategy areas will require a compromise. However, negotiation or working together respectfully to help each partner feel strong is a cornerstone of a long term relationship.

You may have a partner who is not doing what you have asked. First, clarify if your partner understands what you have requested. Give your partner an opportunity to discuss why he or she has not responded to your request. The strategy may require compromise. Perhaps your partner's lack of response reflects a lack of interest or commitment. Or your partner may simply be unable to respond for some other reason. In spite of all the time and effort that you may put into making your relationship work, there are limits to a love relationship. We will be looking at those limits.

There is no substitute for couples devoting the time that is required to have a committed romantic relationship. It takes time to know oneself. It takes time to understand one's partner. It takes time to share and educate each other about the way you want to be treated. However, the outcome of the time spent will be a relationship that is safe and supportive; an outcome well worth the time.

PART THREE

LIMITS OF LOVE

It is time to look at issues that can become road blocks, or non-negotiable topics for couples. A couple may be motivated to work on its relationship and have the tools it needs, yet still be unable to overcome some very basic concerns. These really are the "irreconcilable differences."

DEALING WITH CHANGE
or
LOVE DOES NOT CONQUER ALL

Change is one of the basic facts of life. Couples need to be flexible. Couples have to be prepared to cope with the major changes that occur naturally with life cycles; the introduction of children, changes in financial circumstances, and issues of aging. On a more immediate perspective, couples also need to be ready for unexpected everyday occurrences: the car breaks down, a child gets sick, or the check doesn't clear the bank on time. Each change, whether expected or not, presents a hurdle for a couple to cross.

Frequently, when people feel overwhelmed or stressed by change they become more rigid. They try to "stay the course" and adopt "tunnel vision" simply to feel some sense of personal control. Being too rigid, however, and unable to "go with the flow" can block opportunities and avenues that may support the relationship during times of change or chaos.

When a couple is communicating clearly it is easy to keep the health of the relationship and concern for the partner a priority or central focus at times of change. Although they can't plan for the unexpected and don't have control over change, couples can provide time in their relationship to share and keep their emotional steps coordinated. Too often the couples we work with become controlled by the pace of their lives and can't find time to share. They become adversely reactive to change and to each other. They get out of step and can't meet the hurdles of change in rhythm.

We can't plan for change but we can plan for time as a couple to discuss change.

As we pointed out earlier in this book, most of us are attracted to someone who is very different from ourselves in distinct ways. In order to live with a person who is different one has to be able to adapt, change, and compromise. Flexibility is the ability to adapt to change. Compromise is a necessary part of flexibility. We have found that when we mention the word compromise, a first reaction is "you want me to change and do everything my partner wants me to do." We are not suggesting that people base their lives upon the requests of their partners. We are saying that the needs and concerns of your partner have to be factored into the equation. For those frequent occasions when people want different things, compromise is required to establish a direction that satisfies everyone.

In order to engage in compromise, without feeling resentful or victimized, it is important that each individual in a couple knows what is most important to him or her. Compromise is a "settlement of differences by mutual concession." If you have to concede something, it really shouldn't be the item that is the most important to you. "Trading," which is the non-emotional component of compromise, is a skill that children learn early on with baseball cards, marbles, or whatever is "cool" to collect and trade at the moment. A child may be willing to give up two of something in order to get something he or she really wants. Knowing which card is your favorite is easy. Understanding what is most important to you, or what you need emotionally, can be more difficult. The individuals in a relationship have to be clear about what issues are important to them, and why those issues are important so they can be ready for compromise.

From our work with couples in relationship counseling, we have developed a list of topics that consistently seem to cause problems. Although it is always best for the couple to talk about these topics before they make a commitment, those conversations often don't take place. Even if some of these issues are discussed, the members of the couple often report that they felt as if they were talking about totally different topics. They really never have a sense of resolution as to where they stand as a couple on these issues.

Any given topic can be viewed from several different perspectives. Each perspective may in isolation seem valid. However, to appreciate the full scope of an issue, it must be explored from all perspectives. There is the old story of three blind men trying to describe an elephant. The first blind man felt the elephant's leg and said it was a tree trunk. The second blind man felt the elephant's trunk and said it was a fire hose. The third blind man felt the elephant's tail and said it was a snake. So it is with different topics that couples have to address. Depending on each partner's perspectives and feelings, the issues can appear totally different. We encourage couples to explore the various relationship topics from five different perspectives or angles.

First, we ask that the individuals describe how they thought the topic under discussion would be reflected in their committed relationship or marriage. What were their expectations coming into the relationship about children, careers, finances, leisure time, etc. Before any effective change can occur, it is helpful to know where people began.

"I expected or I thought we would ......"

Secondly, individuals should explore the emotional importance of the topic or issue for them. Many of the topics that cause relationships to stumble appear simple and relatively concrete on the surface, but they often carry deeper emotional significance. Understanding that having one's own checking account is important to a feeling of independence, or that the annual trip to visit the hometown helps one have a sense of personal identity, is the type of emotional value that has to be explored for these issues.

"What _____ really means to me is...."

or

"_____ is important to me because...."

Next, since, the emotional significance of an issue generally arises from some historic source it is useful for the individuals in a relationship to share their background or childhood experiences as they relate to the topic at hand. Very often an individual's rigid stance on an issue can be softened if the background history can be understood and accepted.

"I hope you can understand that...."

If possible, individuals should inform their partner ahead of time how they might react under certain situations in regard to the topic at hand. This perspective brings the discussion back to the present interaction within the relationship. This focus is not suggested to point out negatives about one's partner, but more to give an early warning signal to interactions that might cause friction. When a couple can be alert and work together, unexpected situations can become a source of support and growth rather than a point of argument.

"I react badly when....."

Finally, as in any important negotiation, the "bottom line", or non-negotiable items should be identified as well as the areas that may be open for compromise. If the individuals have shared where they stand on the previous points and have felt understood, there generally is more room for compromise. Often individuals don't feel that their partner understands or values where they stand, so they lock into their position and stubbornly resolve to "hold their own" in the face of the "enemy" rather than see their partner as someone who can help them navigate through life.

"These areas are non-negotiable ... but I am willing to compromise in..."

The topics presented in this section of the book are not in any particular order of importance. Some of these issues are very specific and concrete in nature and some are more subjective, in that they involve the interaction between two people. The relative importance of any given issue will depend upon each couple.

Earlier in this book we introduced a composite couple, Tom and Mary. They have been married ten years, have two children, and first entered relationship counseling because they felt they were "growing apart". We will continue to look at Tom and Mary's relationship to illustrate how issues can become problematic if they are not addressed. We will follow through with Tom and Mary in identifying the underlying concerns and how they might be overcome.

We want to encourage honest discussion within a safe framework. It is never too late for a couple to explore its relationship and discover new avenues to promote trust and safety.

COMMITMENT
or
HAVE WE BOTH TAKEN THE SAME VOWS?

We begin with the issue of commitment, because clearly it is the cornerstone of any relationship. Yet, often it is the underlying cause of "irreconcilable differences." In our work with couples in distress, understanding the role of commitment in the relationship is our first order of business. There are several definitions of the verb, "to commit", in the dictionary. One is "to pledge (oneself), as to a position or an issue." Another is "to give in trust or charge". Another usage defines the verb, "to commit", as "placing in confinement or custody". All three definitions are relevant to relationships.

In asking couples to talk about their commitment we hear comments like, "I married you, bring home a paycheck, I don't run around. What more do you want?" (This expresses a feeling of being placed in confinement or custody.) We also hear, "When I married you I committed my life to you. I gave up my career goals for you and the children. Now you say you don't want me. Who I am is what I thought you wanted." (This reflects a commitment where the individual gave themselves in trust or charge.)

In a healthy relationship the commitment should be a "pledge of oneself to a position or an issue." In fact, there are several positions that one has to be willing and able to commit to. In working with couples we address three levels or stages of commitment. For a relationship to have a firm foundation, we have to start with level one and build the relationship to level three. Taking the levels out of order always creates a shaky foundation.

The first level of commitment is the pledge that one has to make to oneself. First and foremost, the individuals in a relationship have to be clear about who they are as unique people, what is important to them, and what they have to offer. This self-estimation is the precursor to any healthy relationship. An individual's identity cannot be defined solely through a relationship. By its very nature, a relationship is made up of two separate individuals and it is the coming together of the two individuals that define a relationship.

The second level of commitment is the pledge that one person makes to another person. This pledge means that you see and know the other person clearly and can support who that person is as an individual without breaking the first level of commitment to oneself.

The interplay of these first two levels of commitment can be seen in the following example. Joe and Monique first meet in graduate school. They are immediately drawn to one another and begin dating. As their involvement continues, Joe recognizes that his personal commitment to return to his hometown to take over the family business does not fit with Monique's personal goal of becoming a missionary and serving in third world countries. As much as they care about each other, Joe and Monique recognized that they cannot fulfill their personal goals as a couple and will probably have to go their separate ways.

The third level of commitment, if a couple has maintained a clear pledge to themselves and each other, is the pledge to the direction the two people choose to pursue together. This is the commitment to common goals and values. Although relationship goals will change and evolve over time, the individuals in a relationship should at least know they are heading in the same general direction.

Looking at commitment from these three levels makes it easier to recognize the confusion and conflicts that some couples experience. If there is not a clear commitment on each of these levels, then it is likely that at least one of the individuals will feel confined, trapped, or robbed of their sense of identity within a relationship.

Sadly, romantic love is the greatest enemy of clear commitments. Romantic love is a projection on another person of all that we think we want, need, and seek to have fixed. When we proceed with a marriage commitment based solely on the "magic" of romantic love, we are making our partner responsible for who we are. We turn over the first level of commitment (a pledge we should make to ourselves) to someone else. No one should or can fully carry the responsibility of defining another person.

Romantic love also clouds our ability to clearly see who the other person is, so it is nearly impossible to make an informed pledge to be with and support who the partner really is. Too many people have had the experience of turning over in bed and wondering who this person is that they married.

To achieve the most commonly recognized goals of marriage, i.e., to have a partner for life, to create a home, to raise children, to grow old together, require two people who are actively involved. These goals may be fairly straightforward, but no one can anticipate the hurdles or hardships that life may throw in the way. Both individuals need to know clearly that the goals can fit for them and that they can comfortably work with their partner to accomplish these goals.

When Tom and Mary were first married, they had both agreed that when the time came they would home school their children. They felt it was important to provide their children with as much parental involvement as possible. Mary got a job right out of college in the public library. It was a good fit because Mary was interested in literature and community service. Over the years, Mary discovered a real calling in her work as the community outreach coordinator. When the children were born, Mary realized that as thrilled as she was to have children, giving up her career would be ignoring a commitment to herself that was almost equally important. She was able to share her new awareness with Tom. Tom trusted Mary's decision and was committed in his support of her growth as a person. Together they altered their goal of home schooling their children and recommitted to the goal of developing every member of their family, including themselves.

Questions for Reflection:

- If you were going to explain to your partner your commitment to yourself, what would you say?

- What makes your partner different from you?

- What are the common goals that you and your partner have for your marriage?

FINANCES
or
SHOW ME THE MONEY

The financial beginnings of a relationship are not as simple as they used to be. In the past, a young man and woman got married in their early twenties and were launched into married life with wedding showers and wedding gifts supplying much of the early equipment. It is not as simple in today's world. Today, we find many people marrying later or for a second time, often entering marital relationships with less fanfare and with prior debt and obligations.

Most couples come into counseling with issues about money. It doesn't matter how much money a couple has; common themes reoccur simply with bigger or smaller dollar signs. Couples debate about how money is spent, who controls the money, and how much time is spent earning money, just to name a few points of contention. Money is a necessary part of any relationship and it carries a heavy emotional agenda. Let's look at this issue from the five different perspectives couples might have. For many, money is a vehicle to achieve expectations.

"I expected…"

"I expected that you would take care of me and I wouldn't have to worry about money."

"I expected that we would live in a better neighborhood than my parents."

"I expected that we would share most of the money decisions."

"I expected that my wife would keep working after we had kids and we could count on her income to provide a buffer."

"I expected that we would have a house by the time we were 30 and a boat by the time we were 40."

"What money really means to me is..."

"What money really means to me is a sense of security."

"Money is an indicator that I am successful."

"What money really means to me is freedom."

"Money is a way to get people to like me."

"Money is a way to feel powerful."

"Money is a necessary evil."

"I hope you can understand..."

"I hope you can understand that as a child I didn't have money for any luxuries."

"I hope you can understand that my father used money as a weapon."

"I hope you can understand that money was used to control me, whether through my allowance or things I needed."

"I hope you can understand that money governed my parent's life."

"I hope you can understand that I have worked for my spending money since I was 12."

"I react badly when...."

"I react badly when you question me about my use of money."

"I react badly when we do not have enough money to give the children what they want."

"I react badly when I feel you are disappointed about the money I make."

"I react badly when you take for granted how hard I work to provide for us."

"I react badly when you waste our money."

"I react badly when you discount my worry about our bills."

Non-negotiable areas and areas of compromise.

"I don't care what you spend under $200, but anything over that we should talk about."

"I understand your need to make money, but I am not willing to have an absentee spouse."

"We can discuss my working part-time, but I must be home when the children are out of school."

"I believe that we must save some money, but we have to budget family vacations as well."

The major financial issue for Tom and Mary was disclosure of how money was spent. Tom felt that in order to have financial success, he and Mary had to stick to a strict budget. Mary agreed with Tom that for major expenditures of money they ought to stay within a budget. However, Mary did not want to be accountable for each dollar spent or for purchasing a needed article of clothing. As a couple, Mary felt that Tom was trying to control her and Mary's lack of accountability made Tom mistrust her financially. Rather than staying locked in a conflict, Tom and Mary were able to accept the other's point of view and agreed upon a dollar amount for discretionary expenses for which they did not need to be accountable.

QUESTIONS FOR REFLECTION:

- Can you have fun with money or should it always be used in a practical manner?

- If disposable income exists, what do you do with it, spend it or save it?

- Who decides how money is to be spent? Does each partner have an equal say?

- Where do your attitudes about money come from?

- Can you agree on how your children will learn about money?

- Is there anything that prevents you from trusting your partner's judgment about money?

INFIDELITY
OR
WHAT ARE THE SACRED BOUNDARIES OF OUR RELATIONSHIP?

Most couples would state that they want to and intend to have a committed relationship with their partner when they get married. As part of this commitment, they usually assume that they and their partner will be faithful to each other in terms of sexual and emotional involvement. The marriage vows supposedly secure the deal.

Fidelity actually means, "strict adherence to a promise or duties." When a promise of fidelity is present an individual can experience a sense of security and safety within the relationship. Of all of the topics that create problems for relationships, the issue of infidelity is probably the least discussed. Couples don't like to think about it, much less talk about it, because to do so almost seems to call that promise of security and safety into question. We acknowledge that infidelity is often a threat, an accusation, or a weapon of attack in a relationship, but rarely do couples really get down to discussing what exactly infidelity means to them or, much less, what they would do or how they would handle infidelity in the relationship.

Some people would say that you are unfaithful if you have strong feelings for someone of the opposite sex who is not your spouse— even if there is never any physical contact. Some people feel that it is infidelity if you simply spend a lot of time with someone of the opposite sex who is not your spouse. The majority of people feel that infidelity is having a sexual relationship with someone of the opposite sex who is not your spouse. It is very important that couples clarify what constitutes infidelity for them. It is not unusual for one partner to feel that their spouse was unfaithful when the offending spouse does not view their behaviors as grounds of infidelity.

Sadly, infidelity does occur in a large number of relationships. Even if an infidelity is not discovered, a breech of trust and a betrayal of a promise occurs. The ultimate damage of infidelity is to the trust and safety that should exist in a committed relationship. A feeling of betrayal occurs that often makes it difficult for trust to be regained.

We often hear people resort to the old adage that "what they don't know won't hurt them". We don't recommend sharing past infidelities with your partner as a means to unburden guilt. It is not fair to relieve oneself of guilt by creating pain for another. We do, however, try to get people to recognize the damage of infidelity to a relationship even if it is never discovered or revealed. Deception and dishonesty, which are necessary tools to keep infidelity hidden, can erode even the best relationships. There are times when sharing a past infidelity with your partner is the only way to unblock the barriers that deception has created in your relationship. Ultimately, it is important that one is clear about motive before sharing this type of history with a partner.

"When we committed / married I expected that..."

"I expected that you would never seek the affections of another person."

"I expected that you would have an intimate emotional/ sexual relationship only with me."

"I expected that you would never kiss another woman on the lips."

"I expected that you would never have intercourse with another person."

"I expected that you would never care about anyone more than me."

What fidelity means to me is:	**What infidelity means to me is:**
- trust	- betrayal
- honesty	- lack of respect
-reliability	- a loss of love
- permanence and specialness	- that I am not good enough

"I hope you can understand that..."

"I hope you can understand that I experienced unfaithfulness between my parents as a child and I know personally the damage it can do to a family."

"I hope you can understand that in the past, former partners have cheated on me and I can't have that happen again."

"I hope you can understand that if you were with someone else, I could never have you touch me again. It would be a level of betrayal I could never forgive."

"I hope you can understand that I view sex as having nothing to do with intimacy. It is simply a physical need and behavior."

"I get upset when..."

"I get upset when I think you are spending more time with someone other than me."

"I get upset when you don't seem to want me sexually."

"I get upset when you touch other women even in play."

"I get upset when you seem to be staying away from home longer and longer."

Non-negotiable Areas and Areas of Compromise:

In the area of infidelity, we find that couples are generally pretty clear about what is unacceptable or non-negotiable behavior. We find few areas of compromise, because what feels unfaithful to a person simply feels unfaithful and they usually will not change their position.

Tom and Mary's problems in this area occurred when Tom found out that Mary was spending a good deal of time assisting one of the children's male teachers at school. Tom had thought that the teacher Mary was working with was female, and when he found out that the teacher was male, he was upset with Mary. Tom needed to explore his own feelings of jealousy and recognize that he had expectations about how much involvement Mary could have with other men. Mary had sensed that it was best not to tell Tom the sex of the teacher to avoid any hassle. In assuming Tom's reaction she had given him cause to question her. Tom's reaction was more related to deceit than infidelity, and Mary's response was based upon unfounded assumptions about Tom. Tom and Mary had to share more openly their personal boundaries in order to feel safe.

QUESTIONS FOR REFLECTION:

-If your partner were unfaithful would that be the end of the relationship?

-If you were unfaithful in your relationship, would your partner leave you?

-What is your definition of infidelity and what is your partner's definition of it?

-Based upon those definitions, have you been unfaithful?

PHYSICAL VIOLENCE
or
THE WOUNDING OF BODY, MIND, AND SOUL

When people commit to a relationship they normally assume physical interaction will center on affection, play or sexual involvement. Because this seems to be such an obvious conclusion, we find that couples don't talk about what would happen if there were instances of physical violence. Often couples report that while there is no physical violence directed at the individuals in a relationship, items are thrown, walls are hit, and abusive words are hurled. Inappropriate expressions of anger can trigger childhood experiences of punishment or abuse. Sometimes the damage is not seen in broken bones but in fear and the imbalance of power that intimidation causes.

"I expected that..."

"I expected that if we got mad at each other we would control our tempers."

"I expected that at some point you would hit me."

"I expected that we would not break or damage our possessions when we were angry."

"I expected that we would never fight in front of the children."

"I expected that if we had an argument you would not try to physically corner me."

"Violence or physical acting out in our relationship means..."

"Violence or physical acting out means that one of us is out of control with our behavior or emotions."

"Violence in our relationship is a total violation of trust."

"When you become physical I am afraid to be with you."

"Violence or physical acting out means that something is terribly wrong."

"Physical violence makes me want to hit back or run away."

"Violence or physical acting out is unacceptable. It means we are past the point of dealing with our conflict without outside help."

"I hope you can understand..."

"I hope you can understand that I suffered enough violence during my childhood to last a lifetime."

"I hope you can understand that I see violence as an inexcusable act; there is no justification for it."

"I hope you can understand that violence from my father was the only model I had for parenting."

"I hope you can understand that I see the breaking of inanimate objects as violence and being out of control."

"I hope you can understand that any expression of violence on your part brings out rage in me."

"I hope you can understand that when you raise your voice it feels like a physical blow."

"I react badly when…"

"I react badly when you scream in my face."

"I react badly when I see you draw back your hand, even if you don't use it."

"I react badly when I hear you screaming over the phone to somebody I don't even know."

"I react badly when I see the children cringe when you are around."

Non-negotiable Areas and Areas of Compromise:

"I am willing to listen to your anger as long as you don't verbally or physically abuse me."

"I cannot tolerate you being destructive to property. If you feel like you are going to lose control, do something else; go outside, take a cold shower."

"You can complain to me about people who frustrate you, but I am not willing to be around you if you are going to be abusive or totally disrespectful to others, even strangers."

"I agree that we have to be able to disagree or even fight at times, but I am not willing to participate in conflicts where the only purpose is to hurt and humiliate me."

Mary felt that it was inexcusable when Tom got angry and smashed his fist against the wall, including the one time when he put his fist through the wallboard. Tom stated that when he felt really angry he needed to do something physical. However, he agreed that he needed to find a more acceptable physical release. In talking though this issue with Mary, Tom became aware that the physical gesture of hitting an object created fear in Mary because of her childhood experiences. In those times when Tom became really angry he agreed to go outside and take a long, brisk walk. If this strategy proved not to be useful in containing his anger, then he agreed that he would look into anger management courses.

Questions for Reflection:

-What is your definition of physical violence?

-What is your partner's definition?

-If either of you committed an act that matched that definition would that automatically terminate the relationship?

-Have you ever committed an act or been the recipient of an act that could be defined as physically violent? How did that feel?

RAISING CHILDREN
or
LEARNING TO BE COOPERATIVE PARENTS

One common goal of marriage involves having children and raising them in the environment of a loving household. Newly committed couples proceed with assumptions colored by visions of common parental goals and approaches in dealing with children. Similarities in background that often draw us to our partner lull us into thinking that we will be in agreement about how children should be raised. The reality is that there will be differences in the area of child-rearing and those differences ought to be discussed before they are allowed to create confusion in the already daunting task of raising children.

The model an individual has for parenting usually comes from how he or she was raised as a child. An individual's emotional experience in dealing with their own parents or primary caregivers will have more influence on the adult style of parenting than the similarities of background. Couples coming from different types of parenting backgrounds will have to coordinate their styles. This will involve clarification of one's style, communication and compromise about how children are handled. How to deal with disagreements when the children are present, issues of flexibility, control, rules, expectations, and discipline have to be addressed.

The bottom line is that different parenting styles will confuse children. Parents must be able to support each other in dealing with the children. If there is no coordination of styles the child can become confused or feel unsafe with the lack of consistency. As children get older they can also become skilled at manipulating the parents and pitting the parents against each other to try to get their own way on an issue.

"I expected..."

"I expected that we would feel the same way about how to raise children since we came from such similar backgrounds."

"I expected that when I disciplined one of the children you would back me up."

"I expected that when we agree to discipline the children, we do not give in and let them off the hook."

"I expected that you would believe that it is important to teach our children to respect our personal property and possessions."

"I expected that we would use some physical punishment when it was necessary."

"Co-parenting means..."

"Co-parenting means we are able to work together. If we can't agree on this most important task maybe we don't need to be married."

"Co-parenting means having someone to share my joy and pride as a parent."

"Co-parenting means having someone to back me up when I am having trouble dealing with the children."

"Co-parenting means a demonstration of your love and commitment to the family we have created together."

"I hope you can understand that..."

"I hope you can understand that I grew up in a very strict household and will never hold my children to such standards."

"I hope you can understand that I grew up in a household where you could do anything you want and no one noticed. It felt as if no one cared."

"I hope you can understand I grew up with parents whom I could manipulate without much trouble."

"I hope you can understand that the tough discipline I experienced as a child made me strong."

"I hope you can understand that I want our children to feel more loved than I did in my youth."

"I react badly when..."

"I react badly when you don't support me with the children."

"I react badly when I set a punishment that you undo."

"I react badly when you don't show me respect in front of the children."

"I react badly when you make a decision about the children's activities without consulting me."

Non-negotiable Areas and Areas of Compromise:

"Even if we don't agree with each other in a particular instance, we have to support one another and talk about it later in private."

"Neither one of us should change a punishment that the other has imposed until we have talked (at least by phone)."

"There is never a reason to be disrespectful to one another in front of the children."

"If we notice that one of the children is being manipulative, we must deal with it privately and not in front of the child. Keep me informed privately about how you see the children manipulating me."

Tom came from a military family where you were told to obey and keep your mouth shut. Mary came from a very liberal family where she felt that to some degree she raised herself. As adults both Tom and Mary went in opposite directions from how they were raised, so Tom was more prone to give in to the children, and Mary was more determined to stick to the rules. Both Tom and Mary had to work to understand their partner's method of discipline so that the children could not take advantage by playing one against the other.

Questions for Reflection:

-Which "style" of parenting did your parents exercise in raising you? Which parenting style did your partner experience?

-How are you and your partner similar in terms of child rearing practices? How are you different?

-How well do you and your partner support each other in dealing with your children?

INVOLVEMENT WITH FAMILY AND FRIENDS
or
GUESS WHO'S COMING FOR DINNER?

In a healthy relationship we know how important it is for each partner to have strong ties to family and friends. The better individuals can relate to family members and friends, the better they can usually relate to a marital partner. However, problems arise when partners begin to spend more energy or time with family or friends than they do with their spouse.

There may be legitimate reasons for focus and attention on family and friends: sickness, emotional problems, or some sort of special need that exists. Yet, often when people are unhappy with their spouse, they tend to escape from their relationship by spending extra time with their family or friends. In essence they meet their relationship needs, outside the marriage, in a socially approved manner and avoid dealing with their partner.

When one partner travels or is away from home a great deal, the involvement of family and friends can become an issue. The individual at home may understandably look to outside support to fill the gap left by the absent partner. When the partner returns there can be a conflict or a sense of divided loyalties. One partner may not want to cut off their local support base and the "returning" partner may find that stepping into the home routine is difficult because others have been playing their roles.

When there is conflict in a relationship, we commonly find that family and friends are used as a buffer by the couple to avoid being alone with each other. Although there are instances or legitimate reasons for one partner to spend more time with a close friend or family member, at these times a relationship has to be strong enough for the less involved partner to handle the shift of energy and focus away from the marital relationship for a while.

"I expected..."

"I expected that you would spend more time with me and less time with your friends after we got married."

"I expected that we would have privacy in our home and would limit our friends to visiting at certain times."

"I expected that you would understand if my family needs me, I will be there."

"I expected that we would limit family visits to holiday times."

"I expected that our marriage commitment and our family would come first, and your family would be second."

"Involvement with family and friends represents..."

"Involvement with family and friends represents a valuable support base."

"Involvement with family and friends represents just another set of obligations."

"Involvement with family and friends represents a way that we can be supportive of others as a couple."

"I hope you can understand that..."

"I hope you can understand that I was raised with a large extended family and I want the same for my kids."

"I hope you can understand that being with family was painful when I was young and it is not a positive experience for me as an adult."

"I hope you can understand that I feel a sense of obligation to my parents and want to be there for them as much as I can."

"I hope you can understand that I never received much attention from my parents because of their involvement with their friends, and I don't want my children to feel that they have to share me with others."

"I hope you can understand that without friends I will feel smothered in this relationship."

"I react badly when..."

"I react badly when you don't keep me informed about engagements we have with family or friends."

"I react badly and cannot relax because I don't know when your family will pop in to visit."

"I react badly when my family cannot be involved at holiday times."

"I react badly when you think I can meet all of your social needs or that you should be able to meet all of mine."

"I react badly when I discover that you have told your mother things I thought were confidential between us."

Non-negotiable Areas and Areas of Compromise

"I will feel better about the time we spend socializing if we can place a priority on our time alone."

"I don't mind having your family or friends over if I can head back to my study when I have had enough."

"I want us to save the evening hours for our family time. Please try to limit the phone calls from your family and friends."

"I understand that you don't have the same social goals I do, but I want us to have some social interaction with others at least once a month."

"I can accept your travel schedule, but I want you to recognize that my life has to go on when you are not at home."

Tom began to question why Mary's relatives began to spend more time in their home than in their own home. Tom really liked Mary's family as a whole, but he didn't want to "live with them." Mary began to realize that she was using her family to avoid being alone much with Tom because they were not able to be comfortable around each other. As Mary and Tom addressed their relationship concerns in counseling, they were able to schedule time with Mary's family that maintained family contact and support, but did not prevent them from being with each other.

151

Questions for Reflections

-How comfortable does your partner feel about spending time with your family?

-Does your partner have any particular friends that bother you more than others? Why?

-Do you use friends or family to avoid dealing with your partner?

-If there is no family close to where you live, how would you feel if they moved to the same city?

- Are you and your spouse okay with having friends of the opposite sex?

EQUALITY
or
WHO REALLY TAKES OUT THE TRASH?

Ideally most couples would state that they plan to be "equals" in their relationship. Absolute equality, however, is impossible. Everyone who comes into a relationship has different backgrounds, skills, and capabilities. So a sense of equality actually relates more to a mutual understanding of each partner's skills, and a comfort and acceptance of the fact that you are different.

It is difficult for some people to accept that they cannot do something by themselves and that they may need help. Accepting help from the person to whom we are the most vulnerable can be scary. There has to be a level of trust and comfort in the relationship in order to relinquish control.

Surrendering control in a particular area can be more difficult than it sounds. We often work with couples where one partner has given the responsibility for an area to his or her partner yet remained on the sidelines as critic, teacher, or evaluator. When you allow your partner to lead, your role becomes one of support; trusting in your partner to choose the best direction for the family.

Couples need to talk about who can best take the lead in a given area and why. Keep in mind, that strengths, interest areas, and the particular demands of a family change over time. The "division of labor" that worked early in a marriage should be re-evaluated as assets grow, children grow, and other demands enter the picture.

I expected:

"I expected that we would share the main responsibilities as a couple and parents."

"I expected that since you are going to be at home more that I am, you would take more responsibility for the household decisions."

"I expected that you would take more responsibility for those things that require someone stronger and bigger than me."

"I expected that each of us would complete the tasks we have agreed to do in terms of the household and children."

Equality in our relationship is important to me because:

"In my mind, equality is what partnership is about."

"Equality is important to me and I feel manipulated if you try to get me to do your share of the work around the house."

"Equality is important to me and I feel like one of the children if you don't let me do my fair share."

"Equality is important to me and I resent the fact that you try to shut me out of certain areas or decisions."

"Equality is important to me and I feel close to you when we are working on things together."

I hope you can understand that:

"I hope you can understand that I would prefer for you to be responsible for the financial decisions, because I don't have the experience with investments. That is how my parents handled things."

"I hope you can understand that I don't expect to do yard work; my mother never did and it is a man's job."

"I hope you can understand that my father was disrespectful to my mother, so I am very sensitive about being taken for granted."

I react badly when:

"I react badly when I feel that you are using me more as a maid than a mate."

"I react badly when I find that you are not taking responsibility for keeping your car properly running."

"I react badly when it is clear to me that the children value your opinion over mine."

"I react badly when I have to pick out the new furniture we are getting and you only critique what I buy."

"I react badly when you won't listen to my opinion about certain things."

Non-negotiable Areas and Areas of Compromise:

"I am willing to do my part, but we need to agree on the division of labor, rather than you deciding what I should be doing."

"I will be responsible for my roles in the family, but when I need help, I want to be able to ask, without having you assume that I am trying to get out of my job."

"I will take over the responsibility for the remodeling project, but I don't want you to come behind me and second guess every decision."

"I am willing to divide up the family responsibilities, but we should look at the division of labor based upon ability and not typical sex role patterns."

Tom recognized one day that he had little input into the children's activities. He felt he had lost control over his role as a parent. Tom began challenging both Mary and the kids about their routine. Mary did not appreciate his "butting in" the kid's schedule, particularly when he had ignored it for years.

Questions for Reflection:

- To what extent do you feel equal to your partner in your relationship?

- In what areas do you feel your partner has more power than you do?

- Does a "division of labor" occur because of mutual agreement or because you have allowed your partner to determine what your jobs will be?

- What are the areas of strength, experience, or knowledge you bring to the relationship? - What areas of strength, experience, or knowledge does your partner offer?

RELIABILITY and LOYALTY
or
I WANT TO RELY ON YOUR LOYALTY

Reliability and loyalty are issues that frequently come up in relationship counseling. Behind both of these topics is the underlying theme of trust. Individuals need to know what they can count on in their relationships or involvement with others. We combine the topics of reliability and loyalty because loyalty is often the emotional goal people are looking for and reliability is the behavioral expectation that couples seek.

Most people expect their partner to be loyal to them. If we define loyalty as being "emotionally faithful" to one's partner then it is easy to see that this could mean many things to different people. The essence of loyalty, on a very basic level for most people, is the sense that someone is going to be there for you no matter what; that you hold a position of priority and importance in your partner's life. On a feeling level, that may be a desired and defensible expectation, but it may not always be realistic on a practical level. A work deadline, sick children, the illnesses of a parent can make it difficult for the partner to always be "there".

It is important for each individual to be aware of the behaviors and responses that they want, to generate a feeling of loyalty for them in the relationship. This is where issues of loyalty can spill over into the practicalities of reliability. We need to recognize the loyalty that we do get from our partner, and not minimize or discount our partner's commitment simply because that person is not always able to be reliable.

Reliability, which we are suggesting is the action component of loyalty, can be viewed as the need to count on your partner to come through for you, or be there for you, in specific ways. Once again, individuals have to be able to state clearly the important ways they need to count on their partner. Leaving the specific expectations of reliability and loyalty

157

unstated simply sets up problems for both individuals in a relationship.

How often have you said to your partner, "If you say you are going to do something, I need to count on you to do it". This is a common complaint we hear in relationship counseling. Of course, this complaint falls under the category of reliability, but it also raises the question of loyalty. When partners do not do what they tell us they will do, one emotional explanation that we come to is: "I must not be important enough to my partner for them to care about coming through for me."

Situations and circumstances may prevent us from always being reliable. However, if one is able to acknowledge and be honest about the specific ways one may let their partner down, it does not have to affect the foundation of loyalty or emotional trust.

I expected:

"I expected you to be loyal and on 'my side', so that when I am in a disagreement with someone, you would at least not argue against me."

"I expected a request from me would be more important than a request from a friend."

"I expected that when I ask that something be kept private you will not talk about it with others."

"I expected you to do what you said you were going to do."

Loyalty in our relationship means:

"Loyalty means I can count on you to support and help me."

"Loyalty means that we are a team.

"Loyalty means that you will not let me make an idiot of myself in front of others.

Reliability in our relationship means:

"Reliability in our relationship means that you will do what you say you are going to do."

"Reliability means that I can count on you to follow through if I can't do something."

"Reliability in our relationship means order, stability, and efficiency."

I hope you can understand:

"I hope you can understand how I felt when my parents would always take the teacher's side on an issue instead of supporting me."

"I hope you can understand that my mother thought that it was perfectly alright to share all of my secrets with her friends. I was just another topic of gossip over coffee."

"I hope you can understand that I grew up with an alcoholic mother. She would say that she loved me in the morning, but at night I was the last person she wanted around."

"I hope you can understand that since both of my parents are dead, I need to count on you to be there for me. You are my family."

"I hope you can understand that I want to count on an adult partner in ways that I could not count on my parents."

I react badly:

"I react badly when I need a friend and you decide to be a critic."

"I react badly when you say you are going to go to the doctor with me and you don't show up."

"I react badly when I can't count on you."

"I react badly when you make fun of something I did in front of our friends. It feels disloyal."

"I react badly when you allow your mother to criticize my parenting."

Non-negotiable Areas and Areas of Compromise:

"I recognize the importance for us both to have outside support people, but we need to agree on the topics that we will not share with others."

"I don't have any problems with last minutes changes, but you have to let me know as soon as you can. Don't avoid me because you think I will be angry."

"I know visiting my parents is hard for you, but I expect you to be present as my partner. I will support you if you want to return home early."

"I do not want to spend holidays on separate vacations."

Mary was hurt and angry when she learned that Tom had talked with his sister about a recent fight they had. Mary felt that Tom's action was disloyal and he had violated the privacy of their marital relationship. She was particularly upset because he had talked to one of his family members whom she saw on a regular basis. Tom felt that he had done the right thing, when he wanted to vent about the fight, by picking a family member that he knew would protect his confidence and not betray it. As a couple, Tom and Mary should agree ahead of time about the outside support people for each of them. They also need to identify specific topics that are "off limits" for discussion with anyone.

Questions for Reflection:

- What actions or behaviors promote a sense of loyalty in your relationship— for you, for your partner?

- Have you and your partner talked about what would constitute being disloyal in this relationship?

- Which are the most important ways that you need to count on your partner?

- Do you feel that you can rely on your partner to do what they say they are going to do?

THE ROLE OF RELIGIOUS INVOLVEMENT
or
WHAT TO DO ON SUNDAY/ SATURDAY MORNINGS

In any committed relationship there has to be a mutual respect and acceptance of the partner's spiritual and/or religious involvement. Whatever the differences in beliefs and involvements, an individual's belief system is an inherent part of that individual's identity and that rejection or disrespect of a person's religious beliefs becomes a disrespect and rejection of the individual.

An individual's spiritual life can be intensely private and guide their path on a daily basis. One's religious involvement is often more public and social and can be a structured part of an individual's choice of activities. Individuals need to accept their partner's spiritual beliefs and address the role that religious involvement plays in their life as a couple. Ideas about the structure and frequency of worship, religious education for children, religious traditions and rituals are all factors that impact a relationship.

I expected:

"I expected that we would attend religious services together every week."

"I expected that we would observe religious holidays, not just use them as excuses to stay out of work or school."

"I expected that we would raise and educate our children in this religion."

"I expected that a good portion of our social life would include church activities."

"I expected to have my weekends free, without any set structure."

Religious involvement is important to me:

"Religious involvement is important to me as a way to focus my priorities every week."

"Religious involvement is a way to honor what my parents taught me."

"Religious involvement is a way to feel connected with others in worship."

"Religious involvement is important to me as a way of teaching our children the values and principles I think they ought to know."

"Religious involvement is something to avoid. It promotes separation and discrimination."

I hope you can understand that:

"I hope you can understand that church activities were some of the most enjoyable things we did as a family when I was young."

"I hope you can understand that my parents expect me to have a religious involvement and raise my children in the faith."

"I hope you can understand religion was shoved down my throat as a kid without any chance for compromise."

"I hope you can understand that I was not allowed to play with certain kids of a different religion."

"I hope you can understand that my church family is the one constant I know I can always count on."

I react badly:

"I react badly when I feel you make fun of my commitment to the church."

"I react badly when you fall asleep during the sermon."

"I react badly when I have to bring the children to services and don't have your help or support."

"I react badly when some of our friends are not welcome at certain social functions."

"I react badly when my private mediation and communion with things in nature are not considered a form of valid worship."

Non-negotiable Areas and Areas of Compromise:

"I want to have some form of structured worship in our lives, but where we choose to worship is open to compromise."

"I want our children to have some form of religious education; that doesn't mean I expect them to go to parochial school."

"I will not join a religious institution that openly discriminates against certain minorities."

"I will support your involvement with church, but I do not want to feel obligated to go with you every week."

Tom and Mary had never had a conflict over religious involvement. They came from a similar background, were married in the church, and mainly attended services at holiday times when they were first married. When the children were born, Tom and Mary were more regular in their attendance because they agreed that they wanted their children to have exposure to the church. The conflict arose when Tom wanted to attend a larger church that offered more youth program opportunities, and where many of his business associates worshipped. Mary wanted to continue attending their small church because the minister gave sermons that really touched her. They had to work out a compromise based upon their personal and family goals for religious involvement. As a couple they had to learn to be respectful and supportive of each other's religious needs.

QUESTIONS FOR REFLECTION

- How do you and your partner differ in your views of organized religion and attending services?

- What changes have you and your partner had to make to accommodate children?

- Does religion make you feel closer or more distant from your partner?

- How are religious holidays or traditions observed in your home? What is their significance?

- What role does spirituality play in your relationship?

ALCOHOL AND DRUG USE
or
ARE YOU COMMITTED TO A PERSON OR A SUBSTANCE?

Social values, family background, and personal experience are just some of the factors that will affect the role that alcohol and drugs will have in a relationship. It is not uncommon for the early stages of dating to involve various types of drinking or drug use. We want to fit in, look cool and be relaxed. How alcohol or drugs are used early in a relationship can often cloud some important questions and expectations that couples need to address. It is important to note that if one comes from a family where chemical dependency was a factor, the individual is more likely to be drawn to someone who has similar tendencies (the list we don't know) and run the risk of becoming chemically dependent themselves.

The use of alcohol in social settings is a legitimate part of our social culture. Non-prescription drug use is not legal. However, it still plays a role in certain social environments and cultures. Couples need to be clear about the level to which mind-altering substances will be allowed in their relationship. Which substances are acceptable? When can substances be used? Is there a limit to how often substances can be used? How will excess use be handled? Do the limits change around the children?

The use of alcohol or other substances often begins on a comfortable social level. The "high" is relaxing. Many feel that it makes them more comfortable, more sociable, more confident, more fun, more creative, or more interesting. Some people, however, begin to look to the effects of alcohol or drugs for uses other than the occasional social use. It can help them relax and cope with the stress of work, the kids, or just daily problems. They can feel more confident in confronting their partner. They can feel more entertaining and playful

169

around the house on the weekend. The hassle of daily chores is less troublesome. They can have more energy, more concentration, more focus to get tasks done. For some alcohol or drugs can quickly become a relied upon and sought after partner in dealing with life.

If a person has progressed to the stage of addictive drinking or drug use, any relationship an individual is involved in is in jeopardy. This is a strong statement, but a true one. Addiction is a physical, psychological, and social disease. For the addicted individual, primary drives and commitments are directed toward the use of alcohol or drugs. Addictions can be such powerful forces that the individual will sacrifice their health, safety, employment, and relationships to satisfy the addiction. The individual's relationship with alcohol or drugs becomes the most important commitment they have. Healthy relationships are based upon a commitment to oneself and to another. When addiction becomes the primary commitment, the alcoholic/addict is not able to participate in other-directed commitments.

I expected:

"I expected that once we got married and settled down, you would drink less."

"I expected that it would be okay for us to have a drink or two together before dinner."

"I expected that you would be okay if I had a few beers while I was mowing the lawn."

"I expected that you would be supportive of the fact that I cannot drink."

"I expected that we would never have any illegal drugs in our house."

The use of alcohol/drugs represents:

"The use of alcohol represents my adult status. I have earned the right to have some "down" time."

"Alcohol and drugs represent a barrier that keeps us from really being able to relate honestly with each other."

"The use of alcohol is the only escape I get."

"The use of alcohol and drugs represents a lack of self control."

"The use of alcohol and drugs represents nothing in particular. I can take it or leave it."

I hope you can understand:

"I hope you can understand that alcohol was at the center of a lot of terrible scenes between my parents when I was young."

"I hope you can understand that I know all about how you can inherit the alcohol gene, but I will not let that keep me from enjoying a night cap."

"I hope you can understand that maintaining my sobriety and recovery are the most important personal goals I have."

"I hope you can understand that my religious upbringing looked down on the use of alcohol."

"I hope you can understand that your family may have served wine with dinner, but mine didn't."

I react badly when:

"I react badly when you try to control my behavior."

"I react badly when you drink and I become invisible."

"I react badly when you try to plan our day or social activities around the use of alcohol."

"I react badly when you bring marijuana home even though I don't want it in the house."

"I react badly when our children ask what is wrong with you when you have been drinking."

Non-negotiable Areas and Areas of Compromise:

"Driving under the influence is not acceptable. Can we take turns being the designated driver when we go out?"

"I enjoy having a drink as much as you, but we have to agree that a nightcap is the exception rather than the rule."

"I don't mind you having a few beers with your friends, but I do not want you drinking around the children."

"I will not control your choices, but you have to respect the fact that I choose not to drink."

"As much as I love you, I will not bail you out of jail if you get a DWI."

Tom and Mary both enjoy social drinking on occasion with friends. However, Mary feels that Tom becomes overly flirtatious with some of the other women when he has too much to drink. Tom gets angry when Mary "corrects" him at a party, because in his mind he is just having fun. After some discussion (at a time when neither of them have had anything to drink), they agree upon a signal that Mary can give Tom when she believes his behavior is becoming inappropriate.

Questions for Reflection:

- Have you and your partner ever talked about how much is too much?

- What mind-altering substances are off limits in your relationship?

- Do you feel that your partner abuses alcohol or drugs?

- Have you ever been concerned that you had a problem with alcohol or drugs?

- Is there a family history of alcoholism in either of your families?

PERSONALITY QUIRKS
or
WHAT YOU SEE IS WHAT YOU GET

In many relationships one or both people have a distinct personality quality that can become troublesome for their partner. We are referring to those qualities or outlooks on life that can usually be spotted in a person early in childhood. Examples of these traits include being an optimist, being a pessimist, being sensitive, being competitive, being a "worry wart", being "laid back", being meticulous, or being just a "free spirit". Early in a relationship these qualities might seem endearing or refreshing. Ten years into the commitment, that "laid back" approach could get a little old. Some individuals state that they thought they could change their partner or that they would grow out of their approach. Yet these unique personality styles usually don't change.

Acceptance of our partner is the critical factor in whether these "quirks" become a problem in the relationship or whether they simply present an interesting challenge in learning to work as a team. Acceptance does not mean that we necessarily like or prefer how our partner is in all aspects. We need to be willing to be honest with our reactions and work with them on the things we don't like. When an individual feels defensive about their own "personality quirk" they tend to become more rigid. In working with couples, we have found that if a person feels accepted they can be more flexible. For example, if one individual in a relationship eats too fast for their partner it can become an irritating quirk affecting an otherwise pleasant meal. If this quirk can be discussed openly, the couple might reach an agreement that does not demand that the one person eat slower, just that they at least leave enough food on their plate so their partner is not eating alone.

In counseling, we see the irritation caused by personality quirks as a fairly accurate indicator of the tension level in the relationship. When a couple is relating well, these quirks are more easily accepted. A month later, if there is a problem brewing in the relationship, these same quirks are on the front line of attack.

Often there is a reason we are drawn to someone with a particular personality approach. Perhaps we are used to the style because it is like that of one of our parents, or we like it because it is the opposite of our parent's style. Sometimes we are drawn to a quality we wish we had. It is helpful to understand our own reaction to these traits so we can respond to our partner rather than to our own agendas from childhood.

In most instances, people are quite comfortable with their own personal style and don't see a reason to be different. In a healthy committed relationship, we usually find that people are willing to make small adjustments in their behavior if it can make their partner more comfortable. If these "quirks" do not present a danger to others or interfere with an individual's quality of life, then acceptance is in order. In certain circumstances these quirks can become excessive or clearly detrimental. If that is the case, counseling can be useful.

I expected:

"I expected that over time you would become less pessimistic."

"I expected that you would accept me if I accepted you."

"I expected that my love could take away your worries."

"I expected you to get more serious once we had kids and a mortgage to pay."

Accepting your quirks means:

"Accepting how you are means I have to work at not letting your pessimism bring me down."

"Accepting how you are means I have to try not to berate myself because I am not as meticulous as you."

"Accepting how you are means I have to remind myself that I am not being ignored and you do still love me, since your "laid back" approach does not include overt expression of affection."

"Accepting how you are means I have to work twice as hard to make sure I cover all the bases so you won't worry as much."

I hope you can understand that:

"I hope you can understand that I worry because I am afraid something horrible will happen if I don't."

"I hope you can understand that my off the wall sense of humor allows me to break the ice with people."

"I hope you can understand that I feel more relaxed when I have everything in order."

"I hope you can understand that when I look at things pessimistically and don't expect much, I am never let down."

I react badly to your personality quirk when:

"I react badly when you try to get me to worry in a way that is unnatural for me."

"I react badly when you joke around with me and don't stop when it is time to get serious."

"I react badly when you tidy up my desk without asking me."

"I react badly when you try to smash my optimism with your pessimism."

Non-negotiable Areas and Areas of Compromise:

"I can accept your strange sense of humor as long as you can restrain yourself around my parents."

"I can accept your pessimism, but I will not let you use it to avoid things that you need to do; like going to the doctor."

"I know that you will always worry, but please don't make the children fearful of life."

"I can accept your optimism in business as long as you don't endanger us financially."

Mary is a planner. She tries to look at every possible contingency and have a back up plan prepared in all events. For Mary, this type of planning helps her feel safe, and she is actually better able to enjoy activities when she knows she is "ready" for anything. Tom often pokes fun at Mary about this detailed planning. Mary clearly is not humored by Tom's comments. If fact, she becomes even more detailed oriented almost to prove to Tom the value of her planning. If Tom could accept that Mary will simply always be a planner, she would probably be a little more relaxed because she would know that she could count on Tom rather than having to defend herself.

Questions for Reflection:

- Do you have a particular personality quirk that you know annoys your partner? What is it?

- Does your partner have one that annoys you? What is it?

- Have you placed too much emphasis on trying to change your partner's quirks?

- Have you learned to accept each other's quirks?

- What have you tried to do to help your partner be more comfortable with you?

SEXUAL EXPECTATIONS
or
ARE WE IN THIS TOGETHER?

Most couples hope for a passionate, intimate and exciting sexual relationship. The romantic and sexual themes on television, in movies, and magazines encourage sexual expectations. Yet with all the hopes and expectations, the topic of sex remains one of the great unmentionables in a relationship.

Safety is the most critical component in a long term satisfying sexual relationship. Sexual involvement in a committed relationship hopefully means feeling safe enough and trusting enough to be open to your partner on physical, emotional, and spiritual levels. When the sexual involvement in a relationship is used as a tool for control, or as a response to other aspects of the relationship, the intimate bonding of sex is lost.

Honest and open discussion about sex is difficult for many couples. It brings up fears and insecurities that many people would rather not face. However, it is often simply the lack of sharing that creates the greatest problems. Couples should coordinate their sexual hopes and expectations. Although it may not sound very romantic, the sexual part of a relationship requires planning just as the areas of parenting or household responsibilities.

When people are uncomfortable talking about sex, they will usually avoid the topic, respond defensively whenever the topic is raised, or spend money in therapy to discover why it is so difficult. A more successful approach to dealing with one's discomfort with the topic of sex is to simply look at what "conditions" or assurances would make you feel safe enough to discuss the subject. Do you need your partner to promise not to laugh, or instruct, or bring up past lovers? Does it help to talk about sex at the kitchen table rather than in the bedroom?

How comfortable are you talking about this important subject with your partner?

In working with couples, we encourage each partner to identify actions that constitute sexual behavior for them. More specifically, the couples need to understand when they move from an "affectionate" gesture to a "sexual" gesture. This varies from person to person. For some, a particular kind of kiss indicates sexual activity. For others a particular type of touch or hug or comment suggests movement into the sexual area; triggering the associated expectations or feelings of obligation. Couples have to understand that what is experienced as sexual behavior by one partner may not be a sexual invitation by the other partner. If one person gets started down the road of sexual expectations and the other person is on a different path it is easy to see how feelings of pressure and rejection are generated.

Other factors that affect one's emotional openness to sexual involvement are the more practical aspects such as the preferred time of day, the presence of children, required foreplay, frequency, or the amount of time needed to avoid feeling rushed or abandoned. When a couple has a common goal, and each partner is willing to cooperate with the other to increase comfort levels, most of these concerns can be easily resolved.

I expected:

"I expected that when we were married and living together, we would at least make love as often as we did before we were married."

"I expected that we would end up with separate bedrooms like my parents."

"I expected that we would share in the responsibility of birth control."

"I expected that we would explore new ways of being sexual, and that we would grow sexually."

Our sexual relationship means:

"Our sexual relationship means a special and exclusive closeness we can share."

"Our sexual relationship is just one more way I feel I let you down."

"Our sexual relationship means acceptance."

"Our sexual relationship is an opportunity to have fun and try new things. It is a way we play."

"Our sexual relationship is a way I can still satisfy you. It is my defense against aging."

I hope you can understand:

"I hope you can understand how conservative my parents were. It is hard for me to talk about sex without feeling I am breaking the "rules"."

"I hope you can understand that I have never felt good about my body."

"I hope you can understand that the sexual abuse I experienced as a child continues to affect how I respond."

"I hope you can understand that I have always been comfortable expressing myself sexually, but that does not mean that I have had a lot of lovers."

I react badly when:

"I react badly when I feel like an object in bed."

"I react badly when you constantly put me off sexually."

"I react badly when you don't seem to care about what I want."

"I react badly when you wear your socks when we make love."

"I react badly when you use sex as a weapon."

Non-negotiable Areas and Areas of Compromise:

"I know our sex life doesn't stop because we had a baby, but I want you to understand that I just don't feel sexy right now."

"I don't mind sharing sexual fantasies, but I do not want to watch pornographic videos."

"I enjoy the affectionate touching we do, but don't grab my breasts while I am making dinner."

"Teaching the kids about sex is one thing, but dirty jokes are not appropriate."

"I am not willing to accept a non-sexual relationship, however I am willing to talk with a counselor if that will help."

In counseling, Tom raises the concern that he and Mary are not normal in their sexual relationship. Tom thinks that they should be having sex at least once a week. Mary points out that, given all of the factors that interfere with their time, they are lucky to be intimate once every month or six weeks. Tom just thought Mary was not interested. Once they agreed that scheduling a time for a sexual interlude was perhaps a good idea, they could make plans for the kids, build up to their date with anticipation, and feel comfortable that neither of them would have to rush off to work or be deprived of sleep.

Questions for Reflection:

- What are your disappointments about the sexual relationship? Can you share that with your partner?

- How have you responded to your partner's concerns or requests about your sexual relationship?

- If you could have anything you wanted from your partner sexually, what might it be?

HOW TIME IS SPENT
or
RELATIONSHIP TIME MANAGEMENT

The basic cornerstone of time management has to do with setting priorities and goals. Allotting time to these priorities with a clear sense of personal goals allows one to effectively utilize time in the most productive way. Many relationship conflicts could be avoided if couples would apply these same simple time management principles to how time is spent in the relationship.

Counselors encourage couples to communicate and coordinate schedules. We go a step further and ask couples to identify their common goals for various segments of relationship time. Couples need to talk about time devoted to work or career, time devoted to family or extended family, vacation time, weekend time, time devoted to children's activities, "empty nest" time, and retirement time.

Vacation Time:

"I expected that we would spend our vacation time together rather than separately."

"It really makes me feel wanted when you want to spend your vacation time with me."

"I want you to understand that I grew up in a family situation with parents that never spent leisure time together."

"I react badly when you plan vacations without consulting me."

"I don't need to play all the time, but if we cannot have fun together I will lose an important reason I chose to be in a relationship."

Retirement Time:

"I expected that we would both have input into our retirement situation. It really is not just your retirement."

"Retirement means that we will have more time to be with each other and share activities, and not just continue to do things separately."

"What I want you to understand is that my parents never planned for retirement. They both had to keep working and never got to enjoy themselves in later life."

"I react badly when it seems that you don't want to grow old with me."

Bottom line: "We need to plan and discuss our retirement even though it is many years away."

Weekend Time:

"I expected weekend time to be 'catch up' time for chores and errands around the house."

"The weekends are my reward for working hard all week. When you just give me a list of more work to do, I react badly and it makes me feel that you don't appreciate what I have already done."

"What I hope you can understand is that I never saw my parents together even on the weekends."

"I react badly when you seem interested in being everywhere, except with me."

Bottom line: "I need quality time with you when it is available."

Time devoted to Career:

"I expected you to try to balance the time you spend working with the time you spend with me."

"I didn't marry you to feel as if I am living alone."

"I hope you can understand that I spent a lot of time by myself as a kid because my parents were too busy earning money."

"I react badly when I feel your job has become your mistress."

Bottom line: "I know that my job demands sacrifice from both of us, but I hope you can recognize that the extra income is important to us."

Time without children:

"I expected that we would try to provide each other with some alone time away from the children."

"I love our children, but I need adult companionship.'

"I hope you can understand how I felt when I was sent off to boarding school at a young age. I don't want our children to feel that we don't want them around."

"I react badly when I sense that you actually use the children to avoid being alone with me."

Bottom line: "I feel we need to balance our free time between the children and time for us as a couple."

Tom and Mary discovered they had different ideas about the use of vacation time. Mary preferred to take all of her vacation days at one time so she could really feel that she had some time away from the work environment. Tom, on the other hand, wanted to add an extra day or two to weekends throughout the year. He did not like to face the work that piled up if he was gone from the office for too long. Before they were able to reach a compromise solution, discussions about vacations were so tense that they ended up not taking vacations for several years.

Questions for Reflection:

- Can you and your partner share the same vision for retirement?

- Do you enjoy doing chores as a couple on the weekend?

- If you have children, what percentage of free time is allocated to their activities versus your adult activities?

- There are lots of reasons why people work. It is not just a pay check for many people. Can you state the benefits that you receive from your work? Can you state the benefits your partner gains from his or her work?

SELF-AWARENESS
or
UNPACKING THE BAGGAGE YOU BRING WITH YOU

We all enter new relationships carrying reactions, memories, and experiences from our childhood or past relationships. As part of our commitment to ourselves, we need to be aware of the impact of our past and how it might affect us in the present. As part of our commitment to a relationship we need to know if we are responding to our present partner from our past experiences.

Throughout this book we have encouraged you to be more aware of how you would like to be treated in a relationship. Hopefully you found this process fun and enlightening. Sometimes, however, we encounter individuals who resist looking inward because they don't want to change. Self-awareness does not necessitate change, unless you want to change. In fact, the resistance to self-exploration in the present often comes from a reaction to past experience. This is the very issue we ask you to think about. Consider the child whose parent is always asking how the child feels or what he thinks and then uses the child's disclosure to tell him that he is wrong for feeling as he does and demands change. Clearly the child's best defense in this situation would be to simply "not know" what he is feeling.

With self-awareness comes personal power. You are much better able to protect yourself from interactions or situations that create distress. You are better able to communicate what you want and why it is important to you. You can be more appreciative and accepting of your own idiosyncrasies if you understand where they come from, and won't be controlled by reactions that seem to come out of the blue.

To explore how your responses from the past may have followed you to adulthood, consider the reactions or behaviors you developed as a child to deal with frustration. Did you withdraw, endure, have a tantrum, read, play sports, take on the role of caretaker...? Often, the behavioral patterns that we establish as a child to cope with hurt, frustration, anger, or pain stay with us and are still the first response, although on a more adult level. As a child it may have been the best response available to you. However, you have to consider whether that response really works for you as an adult. Another effective way to learn how your past patterns or habits may be influencing your current relationship is to give your partner permission to point out when your reactions are inappropriate to the situation at hand.

Tom grew up in a household where his mother suffered from various illnesses. Often his mother was not able to attend his school or sports events because she was sick. He always had to be quiet when she wasn't feeling well. As an adult, Tom finds himself getting angry with Mary when she is sick. Although Mary's illnesses are much less severe than what his mother had experienced, Tom still responds to his past disappointment in his current relationship. If Tom would give Mary permission to point out to him that she senses his anger when she is not feeling well, Tom could look at the source of his response and consciously work at being more supportive, instead of angry. He must remember that Mary is not his mother.

When she was a child and there was conflict or tension around Mary's house, Mary would retreat to her room and get lost in books. By reading, Mary could escape from the fear she had that her parents would divorce and she could pretend that everything would be okay. As an adult, Mary still retreats by reading when there is some underlying tension with Tom. Although it may be a "safe" retreat for Mary, it does not help her relationship with Tom when she avoids, denies, and pretends that nothing is wrong.

INDIVIDUAL BARRIERS
or
RIDING A TANDEM BIKE ALONE

The topics we have covered in looking at the limits of love are relationship issues that exist between two people. There are some barriers or issues that affect one of the partners in a relationship that will prevent a healthy exchange between the two. These issues can create tremendous hardship and pain in a relationship. We have seen couples struggle for years trying to get to the "root of the relationship problem," when the root actually lies within one of the individuals.

We have covered the topics of infidelity, addiction, and personality quirks. Each of these areas can certainly create a challenge for a relationship. We encourage couples to talk about them early in the development of a relationship. However, if an individual moves to the extreme in any of these areas, and is unable to focus on the common goals of the relationship, then all aspects of the relationship will be distorted and skewed.

If your partner is in love with somebody else, at some point he or she will be confronted (either by you, the third party, or his own internal conflicts) to make choices. Many people choose to remain in a marriage rather than lose "the family" or the benefits afforded by the relationship. However, choosing to re-engage emotionally in the primary relationship is not always a simple matter. When a person falls in love and pursues another involvement, there are major emotional factors involved. The person may need individual counseling to understand why they pulled away from the marriage and what their choices meant to them emotionally and to their relationship. They will need to re-evaluate their commitment to themselves as well as their ability to commit to their partner. Often both partners will require time and individual counseling before they can effectively engage in a healthy relationship again. Anger, hurt, deception, insecurity, and guilt can all create impenetrable barriers.

Addiction to a substance or behavior can pull an individual away from his or her commitment to their partner. Addiction is an involvement that can affect a person's thinking, behavior, and choices in detrimental ways. Addictions can become more important than one's health, safety, or commitments to partners, children, and family. When an individual is addicted, the primary goal becomes securing or maintaining the connection with the alcohol, drugs, sex, or gambling and covering up their behavior so no one interferes with their goal. Relationship problems are usually felt long before the depth of an addiction is reached.

An addict is focused on a substance or activity, the partner of an addict can also become addicted to controlling the behavior of the addict. In "co-dependency", an individual is so focused on trying to manage the behavior of another, that he ends up losing a sense of his own identity and what is important to him. In a co-addicted relationship, the interaction becomes a power struggle.

If the addict begins a recovery program, it will not necessarily solve the relationship problems. We have often worked with couples where the co-dependent partner may sabotage the addict's recovery because the partner only knows how to relate with regard to the addiction. Both individuals will need to learn how to relate to themselves and to each other in a healthy, intimate fashion.

We talked about personality quirks as those distinct characteristics of one's personality. The impact of personality quirks can usually be managed within a relationship if the couple is able to talk openly and be respectful of each other's reactions. Some people, however, are not able to recognize or manage their reactions, emotions, or outlooks. A personality quirk taken to the extreme, that impairs one's ability to relate to others in a healthy manner or engage in life, needs to be viewed differently. If one of the partners in a relationship suffers from some form of psychiatric disturbance, the relationship will not be able to continue in a balanced fashion.

We want to address three forms of psychiatric disturbance that will create an obstacle to any relationship. We are not suggesting that you begin analyzing your partner when they are in a bad mood or labeling them as a way to avoid interaction. However, we have often seen couples that have struggled needlessly with their relationship, blaming each other, when the true interference in the relationship could be easily addressed with individual psychotherapy or appropriate medications.

Mood disorders prevent an individual from responding to stimuli in a normal way. This class of disorders will affect one's ability to think things out in a clear, easy fashion, or make appropriate judgments based upon the presented information. Anxiety, depression, and mood instability disorders can be relieved with proper medication and individual counseling.

A personality disorder affects an individual's ability to maintain relationships. One may find it difficult to feel close to another, be direct with one's feelings or even trust another person. Personality disorders are not something to be cured, but need to be recognized and understood. When individuals can understand how their own personality structure works against them and their ability to relate to others, a relationship can be maintained with acceptance, the development of new skills, and the recognition of limitations.

Psychiatric disorders known as psychosis or delusional disorders cause an individual to have trouble recognizing reality. These disorders are best treated with medication and counseling that teaches survival skills. It would be this type of psychiatric disturbance that would be the most difficult to overcome in a relationship.

DEALING WITH CONFLICT
or
A CONFLICT IS A DIFFERENCE, NOT A FIGHT

Almost every book on relationship has its chapter on conflict resolution. Instead of viewing this section as an overworked topic, consider the importance of the topic if every book covers it. No matter how informed, educated, or skilled a couple is in relating, conflict will occur. It is the one guaranteed interaction in a relationship. In fact we, as counselors, question those couples that report no conflict. Our first question is: "Do you live in the same house?"

People are drawn to others who are different from themselves. As counselors, we encourage the differences and support the benefits that can be gained from different perspectives, backgrounds and experiences. On most occasions the differences add richness to a relationship and the couple can learn to compromise, take turns, or use some other mechanism to manage the differences that occur. Along with the benefits, however, differences can also create conflict.

Conflict in a relationship does not have to mean a fight or even a hurtful interaction. However, in order to avoid the damage that can occur from conflict, the couple has to plan for dealing with conflict directly. If conflict is not dealt with directly, the anger and hurt that underlie it will end up affecting some aspect of the relationship. We often work with couples who are "passive aggressive". This means the anger is expressed indirectly, in a way in which the person can and will deny being angry. The angry message is sent, but there is no direct way to address it. You may know your partner is angry, because they won't talk, take "pot shots" in conversations, "forget" to do something for you, or be cool about sex. However, you do not know why they are angry. It usually is only a short time before you will generate an angry response in return. So both partners are angry, damage is done, and no change is identified or resolved.

Over the years we have worked with some rather angry couples. They come to us saying that they "just can't communicate." Actually, they usually can communicate, with many words, vivid descriptions, and frequently at very loud levels. Listening below the level of accusations, we hear couples arguing about the preventable pitfalls of disagreements. If you find yourself thinking that you do try to deal with conflict but never get anything resolved, then you probably are falling into these same pitfalls. These can rapidly become the focus of the exchange, leaving the original conflict unaddressed.

When anger is the driving force in conflict, the goal of the exchange is often not resolution, but the expression of anger and pay back. Unchecked anger is not very patient or politically correct. For conflict resolution to be effective, anger may need to be acknowledged, but it should not run the show. We have identified some of the more common pitfalls that occur when the expression of anger is unleashed in conflict resolution. The guidelines that follow can help a couple harness the expression of anger and achieve the goal of resolution.

1. Avoid the sneak attack: Schedule a time to talk.

A common complaint in the arena of conflict resolution is the "sneak attack". This is when your partner, seemingly on purpose, raises an issue at the worst possible time. Some favorite attack times are just as you are dozing off to sleep, when all of the children are in ear shot in the next room, when the phone is ringing and the dog wants to go out, just as you are walking out of the door for an important meeting, or in the last five minutes of your favorite show. Generally, before you even get to the issue at hand a new conflict is generated.

If you are a repeat offender of the "sneak attack" you should consider whether you have to generate a conflict just to get your partner's attention. For some offenders, a bad interaction is better than no interaction at all. If you have an issue, approach your partner, inform the partner that you want to talk about a matter and agree upon a time to talk within the next 24 hours. Scheduling a time to talk about a conflict will also help clarify your thoughts and prevent anger from driving the interaction.

Tom had a habit of approaching Mary late in the evening if he wanted to discuss a conflict. By that time, Mary was usually too tired to listen or care about what Tom had to say. She would either cut him off with a curt remark or simply agree to what he said to end the exchange, knowing that she did not mean what she said.

2. Deal with one issue at a time.

It is important to deal with only one issue at a time. It is a fairly normal reaction when someone confronts you with a conflict to respond with your own issue so that you have equal standing. This does not even the score, but only leads to chaos and more conflict. Neither issue will receive proper attention. If another issue comes up in the course of the exchange, set it aside and deal with it after the first issue is resolved, or schedule another time to address it.

When Mary confronts Tom about picking up his clothes, he usually strikes back with his peeve about Mary forgetting to clean out the sink after she combs her hair. Both requests are valid, but one does not justify the other, nor cancel it. To resolve the conflict Tom and Mary need to address both issues as separate and independent concerns.

3. Stay in the present and be specific about the complaint and possible resolutions.

When you have an issue with your partner, be specific about the complaint and use current information or examples. Do not bring in old examples or complaints from last week or last year as reinforcements. We always encourage couples to deal with conflicts within 48 hours. This prevents distortion of facts and the amplification of anger. You also have to remember that conflict resolution is a joint effort. It is unfair to say you don't like something with the expectation that your partner should just fix it. If you have an issue, be specific in describing your concern and the behaviors that go with it. Then, offer possible suggestions or compromises that might help.

Mary gets upset when she sees Tom being self-centered concerning family activities. She can cite chapter and verse for every time he has been self-centered since they were married. When Tom is confronted with all ten years at once, he is overwhelmed and feels attacked. This prevents him from being able to see how he might have been self-centered in the last 24 hours, or how he can do things differently in the future.

4. Avoid negative labels about your partner or his or her family.

It is okay to be angry with your partner, but it is not okay to express that anger in the form of hurtful name-calling. When discussing a conflict, do not call each other names or try to label one another. Do not apply psychological terms or use profane language to describe your partner. Do not speak negatively about your partner's family. Partners may make negative comments about their own family or parents.

However, in the course of a conflict, family references can create an all-out fight with battle lines drawn across bloodlines.

> *When Tom and Mary are arguing, Tom will sometimes express his frustration by telling Mary she is "crazy like her mother". Of course, Mary reacts by defending or counter-attacking. If Tom were to be aware of what is behind these comments, he could more accurately state that Mary's behavior makes him feel crazy and confused.*

5. Avoid bringing in Third Party Reinforcements.
Do not bring in the opinion or comments of others to support your position. These other people are not present and your partner can easily feel ambushed and overwhelmed by invisible attackers. The conflict is between two people; you and your partner. If other people have the same issue, they need to take it up themselves.

> *Mary would often point out to Tom that his friends felt the same way she did about certain issues. The only effect this had on Tom was to make him less willing to work with Mary and more wary of his friends.*

6. Avoid "Mind Reading".
Do not try to tell your partner how he or she thinks or feels. "Mind reading" is a power play. You are assuming that you know your partner better than your partner knows him or herself. In reality you do not know what your partner is thinking. Couples should try to avoid power struggles in conflict resolution. The goal is to work together to resolve a difference. When you start mind reading, you are violating the boundaries

of your partner and not allowing that person to be a separate individual whom you respect.

When Tom and Mary are fighting, it is not unusual for Mary to shut down and not want to talk. This is how Mary responded to conflict when she was a child. Tom, however, driven by his energy to resolve the issue, will tell Mary what she is thinking or feeling, making assumptions about what lays behind her silence. This tactic is counterproductive because it makes Mary feel even more withdrawn and angry that Tom would presume to know how she feels.

7. Listen: Take turns talking, do not interrupt.

Listening is critical in conflict resolution. However, discussions about conflicts carry a certain level of tension and anxiety. When people are anxious or defensive, they tend not to listen. Sometimes they are thinking about their next comment and are not able to hear what has been said. Often, when you disagree with your partner's perspective, the natural inclination is to interrupt and correct. This merely creates more anger and leads the discussion into a power struggle of who is right and who is wrong.

In counseling, Tom and Mary had to learn how to listen, because each of them tried to talk over the other. The counselor had a hard time trying to focus on what either one of them said. They had to learn to focus on what the other was really trying to say, rather than just focusing on their own comments or perspective.

8. State what you heard, make sure it is what your partner said.

It is useful to restate what you hear your partner saying. This ensures that you are listening and not planning your next response. Sometimes our ears work fine, but our brain interferes with what we hear. When you reflect back on what your partner has said, you can use your own words and also try to reflect the intent of what they said. Don't exaggerate, mimic, or be sarcastic. Repeating what you heard also helps your partner feel that they have been heard and that what they wanted to state has been understood correctly.

Tom was sometimes very broad and general in his descriptions of the issues that he had with Mary. Mary found it useful to ask Tom for specific examples about what she had heard. This was useful to both Tom and Mary in identifying exactly what the issues were and the actions that could be taken.

9. Allow a time out.

Respect the fact that your partner may need to back away from the discussion and come back to it at a later time if they feel they are becoming too emotional to hear and respond in constructive ways. Sometimes for safety reasons, a partner needs to back away. This need for safety is essential to achieve a good resolution to an argument. When you press someone who needs to "back away" from the discussion, you may simply escalate the argument and force them into nonproductive and hurtful responses. Interestingly, when a conflict discussion breaks down into an angry exchange, it ends the discussion. Couples have to be open to other safety valves and to be able to back away, for a time.

205

Tom and Mary worked out a system when they were dealing with conflicts. If either Tom or Mary got upset and needed a break, they could put up a hand to signal stopping and take a break for 15 minutes.

10. Put yourself in the other's place.

When your partner is talking to you, try to imagine being "in that person's shoes". The goal of conflict resolution is to bring two differing positions to an agreed upon conclusion. Many arguments could be prevented if partners would take the time to understand the point of view of their spouse. The more a couple can share in non-conflict situations, the easier it will be to remember how your partner might be feeling at a stressful time.

Tom found it useful to try to put himself in Mary's shoes when she shut down emotionally. Remembering what she had shared with him about how she experienced conflict in her home as a child, helped him sense the anxiety and fear that was behind her detachment. When Mary needed to back away from a conflict, Tom could accept what she needed at the time and not take her detachment as a rejection or avoidance of him.

Resolutions come in shades of gray.

As we have stated several times, the goal of conflict resolution is to achieve a common solution from two differing positions. The goal is not to vent anger, or hurt your partner, or prove that you are right. Conflict resolution is not a struggle for power. Couples should keep in mind that no one is totally right or wrong. Disagreements come from subjective perspectives and experiences of two different people. It is important to remember that you do not have to agree with your partner's point of view in order to understand or accept it. Although disagreements may look very black and white, most arguments are resolved with a compromise, in shades of gray.

Once Tom and Mary were able to manage the anger they both brought to a conflict, and learned to listen effectively, they discovered that conflicts were not a problem at all. They were simply a specialized communication that helped them live more happily together.

ISSUES THAT CAN INTERFERE WITH LOVE

LEVELS OF COMMITMENT

FINANCES

INFIDELITY

PHYSICAL VIOLENCE

RAISING CHILDREN

INVOLVEMENT WITH FAMILY AND FRIENDS

QUESTIONS OF EQUALITY

RELIABILITY AND LOYALTY

THE ROLE OF RELIGIOUS INVOLVEMENT

ALCOHOL AND DRUG USE

PERSONALITY QUIRKS

SEXUAL EXPECTATIONS

HOW TIME IS SPENT

SELF AWARENESS

INDIVIDUAL BARRIERS

DEALING WITH CONFLICT

MAKING LOVE SAFE
or
THERE CAN BE A HAPPY ENDING

Love can be safe. A loving relationship can provide support to individuals in achieving personal goals. A loving relationship can help an individual heal past wounds and grow in terms of self-awareness and trust. A loving relationship is the structure in which parents can nurture and provide for children and extended family. A loving relationship can be the vehicle through which couples can reach their common goals for their life together. A loving relationship is where we can find emotional support, permanence, encouragement, affection, honesty, laughter, and closeness. Love can be safe, but it takes time, commitment, awareness, and sharing. We hope that this book, **Making Love Safe,** can serve as a guide to help you and your partner feel safe in the love you share.

About the Authors

Luanne Overton and Philip Guinsburg have been working with couples and conducting professional workshops on relationship counseling since 1976. Dr. Guinsburg is a Licensed Alcohol and Drug Abuse Counselor who practices in the state of Tennessee. He was voted "Outstanding Professional in the State of Tennessee" for alcohol and drug abuse issues and is President of the Tennessee Association of Alcohol and Drug Abuse Counselors. He is the President Elect of the American Academy of Psychotherapists. Ms. Overton has recently retired from active clinical practice, but still conducts workshops and writes with Dr. Guinsburg.

Printed in the United States
23431LVS00004B/280-294